REVISING
BUSINESS
PROSE

THIRD EDITION

REVISING

BUSINESS

PROSE

Richard A. Lanham

University of California, Los Angeles

Macmillan Publishing Company
NEW YORK
Maxwell Macmillan Canada, Inc.
TORONTO
Maxwell Macmillan International
NEW YORK OXFORD SYDNEY SINGAPORE

Editor: Barbara A. Heinssen
Production Supervisor: Betsy Keefer
Production Manager: Jennifer Mallon
Cover Designer: Eileen Burke

This book was set in 10½ pt. Caslon by V&M Graphics,
printed and bound by Arcata/Fairfield.
The cover was printed by New England Book Components.

Macmillan Publishing Company
866 Third Avenue, New York, New York 10022

Macmillan Publishing Company is
part of the Maxwell Communication
Group of Companies.

Maxwell Macmillan Canada, Inc.
1200 Eglinton Avenue East
Suite 200
Don Mills, Ontario M3C 3N1

LIBRARY OF CONGRESS CATALOGING-IN-PUBLICATION DATA

Lanham, Richard A.
    Revising business prose / Richard A. Lanham. —3rd ed.
        p.   cm.
    Includes index.
    ISBN 0-02-367465-2
    1. English language—Business English.   2. English language—
Rhetoric.   3. Editing.   I. Title.
PE1479.B87L36   1992   91-11710
808'.066651—dc20   CIP

Printing: 1 2 3 4 5 6 7   Year: 2 3 4 5 6 7 8

PREFACE

Revising Business Prose differs from other business writing texts. Let me emphasize these differences up front.

1. About *revising*. As its title indicates, it is about *revising*; it does not deal with original composition. Students may agonize about *what to say* but in the workplace this "student's dilemma" hardly exists. The facts are there, the needs press hard, the arguments lie ready to hand, the deadline impends. The first draft assembles itself from the external pressures. Then the sweat really begins—*revision*—commonly done in group settings. Collective revision up through a hierarchy determines the final text for much business writing. It offers the choice leverage for improvement but it needs detailed shared guidance. That detailed guidance deserves a special book. "All writing is rewriting," goes the cliché. Okay. Here's the book for it. It offers a collective writing philosophy which a group can easily and quickly learn to share.

2. Translates The Official Style into English. A specific analytical and social premise informs *Revising Business Prose*. Much bad writing today comes not from the conventional sources of verbal dereliction—sloth, original sin, or native absence of mind—but from stylistic imitation. It is learned, an act of stylistic piety which imitates a single style, the bureaucratic style I have called *The Official Style*. This bureaucratic style dominates written discourse in our time, and beginning or harried or fearful writers adopt it as a protective coloration. So common a writing pattern deserves a separate focus, a book of its own.

3. Rule-based and self-teaching. Because it addresses a single discrete style, *Revising Business Prose* can be *rule-based* to a degree which prose analysis rarely permits. This set of rules—the *Paramedic Method* (PM)—in turn allows the book, with the aid of its accompanying Exercise Book, to be self-teaching. In the workplace, the pressures animating revision rarely permit time off to take a special writing course. You need something useful right then. Again, a special book for this purpose seems justified.

4. Useful in all jobs. Because The Official Style dominates university, workplace, and government, the book can work in all these contexts. The Official Style afflicts us all, a common plague. The third edition of *Revising Business Prose* addresses a common audience of young and old, of barnacled bureaucrats and softshell apprentice apparatchiks, as a single group sharing a common problem.

5. Based on the electronic word. If writing on an electronic screen has revolutionized prose composition and prose style, nowhere has the revolution hit harder than in revision. Revision is much easier to do on screen, more of it will be done, and it will be done in many new ways. Electronic text brings with it a new stylistic theory as well as new means of moving words around on an expressive surface. I have tried to infuse the third edition of *Revising Business Prose* with an awareness of this new writing medium.

6. Saves time and money when used as directed. The bottom line, short and long term: the Paramedic Method, when used as directed, saves time and money. Lots of it. The Lard Factor of The Official Style usually runs about 50%. Just add up everything the written word costs you for a year, time and materials, and divide by two. That figure will guestimate pretty well the savings *Revising Business Prose* can generate. But the book has an even larger end in view—stylistic self-consciousness. This verbal self-awareness, however generated, is like riding a bicycle. Once learned, never forgotten. And stylistic self-consciousness changes how we read and write not only in a single bureaucratic register but across the board. From a particular focus, this book aims to teach a general skill with words. And to suggest that such a skill has moral implications, implications I have dealt with in the last chapter, "Why Bother?"

7. Sentence-based. I save this point for last because it is the most important. *Revising Business Prose* focuses on the single sentence. Get the basic architectures of the English sentence straight, I think, and everything else will follow. We're analyzing in this book the microeconomics of prose. All our work together will be close-focus writing and what acousticians call *near-field listening.* Such close-focus work is as seldom performed as it is universally needed. We spend a great deal of time worrying about our verbal p's and q's that we ought to spend worrying about our sentence architecture. That's where the big misunderstandings occur.

I've called my basic procedure for revision the Paramedic Method because it provides emergency therapy, a first-aid kit, a quick, self-teaching method of revision for people who want to translate The Official Style, their own or someone else's, into plain English. But it is just that—a first-aid kit. It's not the art of medicine. As with paramedicine in underdeveloped countries, it does not attempt to teach a full body of knowledge but only to diagnose and cure the epidemic disease. It won't answer, though at the end it addresses, the big question: having the cure, how do you know when, or if, you should take it? For this you need the full art of prose medicine.

The only real cure for America's literacy crisis is a mature and reflective training in verbal self-awareness. Once you have this, you'll see and correct ordinary mistakes almost in passing. If you don't have it, no amount of rule memorization will produce good prose. For prose style, like the rest of human experience, is too various to be adequately described by rules. (I've addressed this larger stylistic domain in another book, *Analyzing Prose,* which can profitably be read as a sequel to this one.) We don't write by rule but by imitation—as you've no doubt discovered when you've found yourself producing The Official Style. People often argue that writing cannot be taught, and if they mean that inspiration cannot be commanded nor laziness banished, then of course they are right. But stylistic analysis—revision—is something else, a method, not a mystical rite. How we compose—pray for the muse, marshal our thoughts, find willpower to glue backside to chair—these may be idiosyncratic, but revision belongs to the public domain. Anyone can learn it.

The best introduction to the book *Revising Business Prose*, especially if you are working in a group, is the half-hour video of the same name, also available from Macmillan. Start by viewing that. The whole book should be presented on an interactive videodisc and perhaps in the future it will be, but until then even a passive videotape shows writing to be a process whose interior dynamics the printed page can but imperfectly express. And some readers have found that my voice on the tape helps animate the print.

To get the most out of *Revising Business Prose*, use *The Revising Business Prose Self-Teaching Exercise Book* which accompanies it. Don't cheat and look at the answers; do the revisions first. I've provided exercises for several levels of audience. Do them all. Prose revision is an interactive process *par excellence*, and interaction can occur in a print medium only by filling in the blanks. Do it. And follow the Paramedic Method. It works only if you *follow* it rather than *argue* with it. When it tells you to get rid of the prepositional phrases, get rid of them. Don't go into a "but, well, in this case, given my style and my company, really I need to . . ." bob and weave. You'll never learn anything that way. The Paramedic Method constitutes the center of this book. Use it. It is printed on both the inside front cover of the book and on a separate page in the front. Clip it out and tack it above your desk for easy reference.

I've provided an Appendix which defines the key terms used in the text and an Index which makes using the text as a reference easy.

R. A. L.

For their assistance in the preparation of this edition, I would like to thank the following reviewers: Roger N. Conaway, University of Texas, Tyler; John Cooper, University of Kentucky; Judi Gaitens, North Carolina State University; David A. Jolliffe, University of Illinois at Chicago; Carolyn R. Miller, North Carolina State University; Gerald P. Mulderig, DePaul University; Virginia M. Sullivan, SUNY Farmingdale.

In this book, as in all my work, the editorial and scholarly eye of my wife, Carol Dana Lanham, has spared both reader and author many inconsistencies, gaffes, and stupidities. *Gratias Ago.*

CONTENTS

REVISING
BUSINESS
PROSE

THE PARAMEDIC METHOD

1. Circle the prepositions.
2. Circle the "is" forms.
3. Ask, "Where's the action?" "Who's kicking who?"
4. Put this "kicking" action in a simple (not compound) active verb.
5. Start fast—no slow windups.
6. Write out each sentence on a blank sheet of paper and mark off its basic rhythmic units with a " / ".
7. Read the passage aloud with emphasis and feeling.
8. Mark off sentence lengths in the passage with a " / ".

CHAPTER 1

WHO'S KICKING WHO?

What should business writing be like? It ought to be fast, concrete, and responsible. It should show *someone acting*, doing something to or for someone else. Business life offers few occasions for the descriptive set piece; it chronicles history in the making, depicts someone working on matter or with people. It seldom relates abstract concepts for the fun of it; abstractions occur as parts of a problem to be solved. Business prose ought, therefore, to be *verb-dominated* prose, lining up actor, action, and object in a causal chain and lining them up fast.

Increasingly, though, business prose is moving in just the opposite direction, toward a special language we might call *The Official Style*. The Official Style is the language of bureaucracies, of large organizations; it is a noun-centered language, full of static abstractions, voiced always in the passive, and slow. Above all, it strives to *disguise the actor*, allow such action as cannot be quashed entirely to seep out in an impersonal construction—never "I decided" but always "It has been decided that. . . ."

It isn't hard to see why The Official Style threatens to conquer the business world as it has done the government. We are all bureaucrats these days, or shortly will be, whether we work for the government directly or soldier on in the private sector and get our government money through grants, contracts, or subsidies. And even if—especially if—we belong to that shrinking part of the private sector that remains really private, we'll be for certain filling out government forms, having OSHA for lunch whether we invited her or not.

Thus we all have to do business in The Official Style—Federalese, Bureaucratese, Sociologese, Educationese, Doublespeak, or only our firm's "company style." And to do business in it, we will often—though not always—want to translate it into English. If "initiation of the termination process is now considered appropriate" re us, we must know that it's time to look for another job. And some of us may also practice this kind of translation in the name of business efficiency, verbal aesthetics, or plain cultural sanity.

And, as a final indignity, we toil in a society so fond of lawsuits that we want to write everything in legal language—or at least in language that *sounds* legalistic, just to cover our own backsides in the likely event that, somewhere down the line, we'll get sued. But, in a double-bind strategy that would do credit to the IRS, the government also nowadays passes plain-language laws which prohibit writing the kind of defensive legalistic doubletalk that the government itself retails by the cubic ton.

In trying to escape from this maze, we'll begin with some nuts-and-bolts details of sentence shape, rhythm, and emphasis, and then try to focus on The Official Style as a whole, ask what it is and does and why it came about. Next, we'll consider the changes which come when you write on an electronic screen. Then we'll work through a case study that shows the perils of prose revision in a bureaucracy. Finally, we'll consider briefly the central question—when to use The Official Style and when to leave it alone.

WHERE'S THE ACTION?

No responsible businessperson these days would feel comfortable writing simply "Jim kicks Bill." That would be too direct, almost unfeeling, gross. No, the system prompts us to write something like "One can easily see that a kicking situation is ongoing between Jim and Bill." Or, "This is the kind of situation in which Jim is a kicker and Bill is a kickee." Jim cannot enjoy giving Bill a good boot; no, for official use, it must be "Jim is the kind of individual who enjoys participation in an interactive kicking situation re Bill." Absurdly contrived examples? How about these real ones:

> Short-term planning is foremost in the prioritization of the planning loop.

> This is based on the contention that a legal action against a foreign company for the profit under contention would not be a wise move.

> The company is also experiencing a trend of management relocation refusals and a diminished work ethic philosophy among hourly employees.

See what they have in common? They all *hide their central actions* as if they were ashamed of them. In the first example, the "prioritization of the planning loop" must mean just "planning," revealing, as so often in The Official Style, a plain tautology: "Short-term planning comes first in the planning of our planning." Once we eliminate the double repetition, the action comes clear:

> Short-term planning *comes first.*

And we have reduced 12 words to 5, a Lard Factor of 58%. We shall use the Lard Factor as a rough numerical approximation of success in revision. You find it by dividing the difference between the number of words in the original and the revision by the number of words in the original—in this case

$$12 - 5 = 7 \div 12 = .58 \text{ or } 58\%$$

In your revisions, try for a LF of 50%, plus or minus 5%.

Now for the second example. What central *action* lurks beneath:

> This is based on the contention that a legal action against a foreign company for the profit under contention would not be a wise move. (25 words)

Suing. Buried in a noun phrase—"legal action." And what would this action be? *Unwise.* Here, The Official Style has shied away from both *action* and *consequence.* Let's revise to bring them back up front:

> Suing a foreign company for this profit would be unwise.

The beginning and ending of a sentence form natural opportunities for emphasis and the revision seizes them. And we have also emphasized the third element in the sentence drama—"the profit under contention." Simply call it "this profit" and place it mid-sentence and you have a sentence shape which enhances its meaning. And, above all, you have an *action* and a *result of that action*:

> **Suing** a foreign company *for this profit* would be **unwise**. (LF 60%)

And our third example of hidden action?

> The company is also experiencing a trend of management relocation refusals and a diminished work ethic philosophy among hourly employees. (20 words)

You can almost see the writer flinch from the harsh reality. Behind "The company is also experiencing a trend of management relocation refusals" we find an embarrassing subject and verb: "Increasingly, **management refuses** to relocate." And behind "a diminished work ethic philosophy among hourly employees" an even more distressing truth: "and our workers refuse to work." An easy parallelism between the two makes the point even clearer—and more awkward to admit:

> Our managers **refuse to relocate** and our workers **refuse to work.** (11 words; LF 45%)

Our whole culture these days is built on euphemism, on dodging home truths or smearing makeup on them. The Official Style, by hiding the sentence's natural subject and verb in a swamp of nominal constructions and prepositional phrases, allows us to play *Let's Pretend*. It's not a very good game for business but it is played a lot. To escape it, ask, "Where's the *action?*" Somebody's doing something to someone else. Who? *Who's kicking who?* (I know it should be *whom* but doesn't it sound stilted?)

THE "BLAH BLAH *IS THAT*" OPENING

All right. The Official Style euphemizes by hiding the action. It has also patented two more debilitating stylistic formulas, the prepositional-phrase string and the slow windup. Let's look at the slow windup first. We'll christen it the "Blah blah *is that*" formula. Some specimens from my collection:

> What I would like to signal here *is that* . . .
>
> My contention *is that* . . .
>
> What I want to make clear *is that* . . .
>
> What has surprised me the most *is that* . . .

The upshot of what Jones says here *is that* . . .

The first *is that* . . .

The point I wish to make *is that* . . .

What I have argued here *is that* . . .

My opinion *is that* on this point we have only two options . . .

My point *is that* the question of . . .

The fact of the matter *is that* . . .

It's a snap to fix this pattern; just amputate it. Eliminate the mindless preludial fanfare. Start the sentence with whatever follows "Blah blah *is that*. . . ." On a word processor it couldn't be simpler: do a global search for the phrase "is that" and revise out the offending phrase each time.

By amputating the fanfare, you *start fast*. And a fast start may lead to major motion. That's what we're after. Finding the *action*.

> *Despite the fact that* many truckers feel the railroads cannot cut substantially into freight hauls that have belonged to trucks for years, the rails are doing it. (27 words)

> Although many truckers think railroads cannot cut into established truck hauls, they are doing it. (15 words; LF 44%)

The real action here lies in *they are doing it*; the quicker we get there, the better. Another easy amputation:

> Since it is the case that construction is soon to be finished on the $50 million Lovenest Hotel building . . . (19 words)

> Since the $50 million Lovenest Hotel is nearly finished . . . (9 words; LF 53%)

PREPOSITIONAL-PHRASE STRINGS PLUS "IS"

The prepositional-phrase strings usually pose a more complex challenge than the "Blah blah *is that*" opening. Here's a typical string:

> The tremendous growth was mainly a result of the increase of disposable income of people, increased leisure time, and better equipped resort areas catering to all types of skiers.

The worst prepositional-phrase strings are the "of" phrases coupled, as always, with an "is" form, the weakest verb form of all:

> The tremendous growth **was** mainly a result
> *of* the increase
> *of* disposable income
> *of* people,
>   increased leisure time,
>   and better equipped resort areas catering
> *to* all types
> *of* skiers.

Notice how boring and monotonous that string of prepositional phrases becomes? And where's the *action*? "Growth"? "Increase"? "Equipped"? "Catering"? The sentence wants to describe a causal process, as so much of business writing does. What *caused* A? How get from A to B to C? The Official Style always does its best to obscure a causal pattern or a chain of command. Let me emphasize what The Official Style obscures:

> More disposable income, more leisure time, and better resorts, all increased the market for ski accessories. (LF 45%)

The *action* lies hidden in *increased*. Can we find a more powerful verb for this action? Every word processing program has a thesaurus. As synonyms for "increased," mine yields "expanded, amplified, developed, enlarged, augmented, boosted, built, heightened, snowballed, hiked, and raised," among others. Take your choice. Action verbs should stand at the center of business writing. You should always know who is acting, how, when, and toward whom. An electronic thesaurus offers an almost instantaneous choice of action verbs. Use it.

Another easy way to use your word processor: use the global search to find every "to be" form—or even just search for "is." Every time you find one, ask yourself where the action really resides in that sentence, and try to find, via the thesaurus method, a *verb* to express it.

THE PARAMEDIC METHOD

We now have the beginnings of the Paramedic Method (PM):

1. Circle the prepositions.
2. Circle the "is" forms.
3. Ask, "Where's the action?" "Who's kicking who?"
4. Put this "kicking" action into a simple (not compound) active verb.

Now, let's take this search for actor and action, for a detectable and responsible *chain of command* in a sentence, one step further.

After reviewing the research and in light of the relevant information found within the context of the conclusions, we feel that there is definite need for some additional research to more specifically pinpoint our advertising and marketing strategies.

8

The standard formula: "is" + prepositional phrases fore and aft. And often, as here, a "to" infinitive sign joins the conga line.

> *After* reviewing the research and
> *in* light
> *of* the relevant information found
> *within* the context
> *of* the conclusions,
>   we feel that there **is** definite need
> *for* some additional research
> *to* more specifically pinpoint our advertising and marketing
>   strategies.

Who's kicking who here? Well, the kicker is obviously "we." And the action? *Needing*, here buried in *there is definite need.* . . . So the core of the sentence emerges as "We need more research." Let's revise what comes before and after this central statement.

~~After reviewing the~~ (of previous) research ~~and in light of the revelant infor-~~ ~~mation found within the context of~~ the conclusions, ~~we feel that~~ suggest ~~there is definite~~ that we need ~~for some additional~~ more research to ~~more spec-~~ ~~ifically~~ pinpoint our advertising and marketing strategies.

The revision then reads:

> The conclusions of previous research suggest that we need more research to pinpoint our advertising and marketing strategies.

Eighteen words instead of 38—LF 53%. Not bad—but wait a minute. How about "the conclusions of"? Do we really need it? Why not just

> Previous research suggests that we need more research to pinpoint our advertising and marketing strategies. (LF 60%)

And this revision, as so often happens, suggests a further and more daring one:

Previous research ~~suggests that we need more research~~ **has failed** to pinpoint our advertising and marketing strategies. (LF 71%)

By now, of course, we've changed kicker and kickee and, to an extent, the meaning. But isn't the new meaning what the writer really wanted to say in the first place? A previous failure has generated a subsequent need? And the new version *sounds* better, too. The awkward repetition of "research" has been avoided and we've finally found the real first kicker, "previous research," and found out *what it was doing*—it "failed." We can now bring in the second kicker in an emphatic second sentence:

Previous research has failed to pinpoint our advertising and marketing strategies. *We need to know more.*

No "is," no prepositional phrases, an LF of 58%, and the two actors and actions clearly sorted out. The drill for this problem stands clear. Circle every form of "to be" (e.g., "is," "was," "will be," "seems to be") and every prepositional phrase. Then find out who's kicking who and start rebuilding the sentence with that action. Two prepositional phrases in a row turn on the warning light, three make a problem, and four invite disaster. (As you read on, see how many times you catch me disregarding my own advice, and revise accordingly.)

With a little practice, sentences like

The role of markets is easily observed and understood when dealing with a simple commodity such as potatoes.

will turn into

A simple commodity like potatoes shows clearly how markets work. (LF 44%)

ACTION PROGRAMS AND WASTING MONEY

Every sentence describes an action program. To stay in business, you must not lose sight of *what's happening*, who is doing what to whom. Here is a short sentence that manages to blur every important action:

> The trend in the industry is toward self-manufacture by some companies of their own cans, and packing technology is changing packaging requirements so as not to require the typical heavy metal can.

First, notice that the sentence falls into two unrelated parts:

1. The trend in the industry is toward self-manufacture by some companies of their own cans

and

2. packing technology is changing packaging requirements so as not to require the typical heavy metal can.

The two parts must bear some relation to each other; if not, why do they share the same sentence? What might it be? In cases like this, best to find the action in each half and then guess at the relationship between them.

So, the first half. Where's the *action*? Hidden down there in *self-manufacture*. Somebody is *making* something. Who is doing it? Who is the subject? We have a choice of three: *trend, industry, companies*. Easy to see the natural subject here: *companies*. We now have a clear action program:

> Some companies make their own cans.

We know where the action is, who is kicking who. The dead-rocket opening, *The trend in the industry is toward = now*, and so we have

---

11

Some companies now make their own cans. (LF 53%)

The LF of 53% only begins to tell the story. The writer could not express a basic simple action, could not see who was acting or what the action was. And the stumbling approximation took twice as long. Am I overemphasizing a trivial mistake? Suppose your company could save 50% of everything you spent on the written word, from paper and ink to fax machines and employee time? And what of the mental processes of someone who cannot see, or explain, a simple business process? The idea of a *company* should pose no special intellectual challenge to a businessperson. Nor should *making*, nor even *cans*. We're not talking about quantum theory here. The gigantic wastage revealed by such a sentence (or half a sentence—we are far from finished with it) comes in the *thinking* revealed. Thinking time costs a lot of money.

Now for the second half of the sentence.

2. packing technology is changing packaging requirements so as not to require the typical heavy metal can.

Again, who's kicking who? Where is the *action*? The writer tips us off by his redundancy: *requirements* and *requires*. OK, we have a verb—*requires*. Who or what is doing the requiring? Not, as the writer writes it, the *requirements*, since that means that the *requirements* are *requiring*, which is tautological and witless. No, our actor is *technology*. Now, finally, at last, we have actor and action: *packing technology requires*. So we come to this:

packing technology no longer requires a heavy metal can. (LF 44%)

At this point, we can contemplate the relationship between the two halves of the sentence. Since the writer did not specify a relationship but merely juxtaposed the two parts, we must guess. My guess:

Since packing technology no longer requires a heavy metal can, some companies now make their own.

Our Lard Factor, as chance would have it, scores a bull's-eye: 50%, 16 words instead of 32. But, again, the LF only uncurtains the problem. Prose models thought, and thought must account for events and the causal relationships between them, the causes and results that keep a business solvent. The Official Style attacks business at its heart—a knowledge of *what's happening.*

THE PM *SUPER-SLIM WEIGHT LOSS PROGRAM*

Now let's look at a longer and different kind of example:

> Along with the population, the economy should also continue to grow slowly. This is based on three assumptions: First, the tourism industry is becoming saturated, and should not grow at its past rate. Second, state government, which grew rapidly in the past, cannot be expected to grow at its historical rate. And third, for reasons mentioned earlier, it is not likely that manufacturing could become important enough to provide substantial growth. (71 words)

The problem here? Pure lard. The writer sees the bones of action but they are covered by rolls of fat. Let's cut it out. I'll embolden the bones to clarify structure:

> Along with the **population**, the **economy should** also **continue to grow slowly.** This is based on three assumptions: First, the **tourism** industry **is becoming saturated**, and should not grow at its past rate. Second, **state government**, which grew rapidly in the past, **cannot be expected to grow at its historical rate.** And third, for reasons mentioned earlier, it is **not likely that**

manufacturing could become important enough to **provide substantial growth**.

Now, from bones to skeleton:

population & economy should continue to grow slowly

Why?

    tourism saturated

    state government growth slowing

    manufacturing growth slowing

Out of these dead bones, two living sentences tied together by a crucial phrase—*but slowly*—which implies a *causal relationship* between the two.

> Population and economy should continue to grow, but slowly. Tourism is becoming saturated, and state government and manufacturing cannot be expected to sustain past growth rates. (26 words; LF 63%)

Now for something completely different. In recent years, ordinary business writing has become so infected by The Official Style that a new scholarly specialization has emerged to teach business writing. Teachers working in this field must publish articles just like other academics, and these articles must be acceptable to two groups devoted to The Official Style—the MBA types and the empirical linguists. Not only how business is done but how it is studied now goes forward in The Official Style. This "*about-business* writing" hides actor and action under a slime of passives, prepositions, verbs made into nouns, and Latinate "shun" words—institu*tion*alized, organiza*tion*s, configura*tion*s. The resulting prose looks like this:

> With respect to institutionalized properties of organizations, our framework suggests that over time, the actions exercised by

humans in the domains of media use, message structure, and language become habitual, and particular configurations of media, message structure, and language emerge and are invoked in certain circumstances to achieve some communicative intent.

Action? Action? Actor? Actor? What are they talking about? Let's call up the PM *Super Slim* plan and try to find out:

1. Circle the prepositions.
2. Circle the "is" forms.
3. Ask, "Where's the action?" "Who's kicking who?"
4. Put this "kicking" action in a simple (not compound) active verb.
5. Start fast—no slow windups.

OK, we invoke rules 1 and 2:

With respect *to* institutionalized properties *of* organizations, our framework suggests that *over* time, the actions exercised *by* humans *in* the domains *of* media use, message structure, and language **become** habitual, and particular configurations *of* media, message structure, and language emerge and **are** invoked *in* certain circumstances *to* achieve some communicative intent. (51 words)

Now, rule 3. Who is kicking who? Where's the *action*? It's almost impossible to see, but the sentence does contain two centers of power and we can start there:

actions become habitual

configurations of media emerge and are invoked

In these two centers of power lurk five possible actions:

act
habituate

15

configure
emerge
invoke

Now let's translate, or try to, the individual phrases from The Official Style into English:

institutional properties of organizations = company habits

actions exercised by humans in the domains of media use, message structure, and language become habitual
= people tend to express themselves in habitual ways

particular configurations of media, message structure, and language emerge and are invoked in certain circumstances to achieve some communicative intent
= people tend to express themselves in habitual ways

Have I done the passage an injustice? I don't see how. The plain English for the whole passage, so far as I can see, must run something like:

In large organizations, people tend to express themselves in habitual ways. (11 words; LF 78%)

You might then specify what those ways, those media, are. But you would have to name names, have specific actors performing specific actions, people writing, speaking, using E-mail, following accepted report forms, whatever.

Anybody who has studied the social sciences has read acres of such prose. It may be all right for that kind of thinking—though I do not think so—but for business? As an example of business prose, I find a passage like this *scary*. It muddles the world of affairs, a place where *actions* and their *actors* must be clear, and the causal relationships between them precise. If this kind of prose represents how we do business, or think about doing it, no wonder the Japanese keep coming in first.

THE PM SUPER SLIM TAKES TIME

Yes, of course PM revision is tedious and time-consuming. But that only shows the magnitude of the problem. If business writing presents puzzles on the one hand and pretentious flapdoodle on the other, we'll never get any business done. Deciphering such prose is possible, though, and using the PM, you'll soon be doing it quickly. Isn't getting on with your business twice as fast worth the effort? In working, as in the rest of life, it's a big help to know where the action is, who's really kicking who. Nobody in his or her right mind *wants* to write prose like that we have exemplified here. Why keep tolerating it?

In the next chapter, we move from *action* to *sentence shape*. But before that, again, the PM rules thus far:

1. Circle the prepositions.
2. Circle the "is" forms.
3. Ask, "Where's the action?" "Who's kicking who?"
4. Put this "kicking" action in a simple (not compound) active verb.
5. Start fast—no slow windups.

CHAPTER 2

SENTENCES
AND
SHOPPING
BAGS

The Official Style, then, builds its sentences on the verb "to be" plus strings of prepositional phrases fore and aft; it buries its verbal action in nominative constructions with the passive voice; it often separates the natural subject from the natural verb, actor from action, by big chunks of verbal sludge; it cherishes the long windup, the slo-mo opening. Add all these attributes together and you build a sentence that has no natural shape or rhythm, no skeleton to support its meaning. Instead, you get a shopping bag that the writer stuffs with words, using the generative formulas just enumerated. This shapelessness makes Official Style sentences unreadable; read one of them aloud with gusto and emphasis and you feel silly. Try reading this aloud:

The appliance industry has been victimized by a compression factor which resulted in an increase in units manufactured (units were also being continuously upgraded with options as standard equipment) coupled with a negative disproportionate rise in prices.

Reading prose aloud, not speed-mumbling it but using an actor's care, can tell you a lot about sentence shape. So can another simple technique. Take your sentence and write it by itself on a card or sheet of paper. A little wasteful on paper, this technique costs nothing on a word processor. Just open a new file and focus your sentence mid-screen. Try to sketch its architecture, to chart its lines of force. If your word processor permits it, box the selection to further frame your attention. Use your art-paint program to draw abstract shapes that reflect its meaning: a rising line can indicate climax, a falling one the reverse; boxes of various sizes can show relative emphases; changing type font and size can help locate actor and action. Use anything, however humble and unscientific, that helps you *look at sentence shape.*

SHAPING-UP EXERCISE

Let's try it with the sentence just quoted. First, we give it a file to itself. Then we mark off its basic rhythmic units (i.e., noun phrases, verb phrases, prepositional phrases, and other basic units that together build the sentence shape and rhythm).

The appliance industry / has been victimized / by a compression factor / which resulted / in an increase / in units manufactured / / (units were also / being continuously upgraded / with options / as standard equipment) / coupled with / a negative disproportionate rise / in prices.

Maybe a diagram would help. Easy, just a "Return" after each phrase gives us a new, vertical perspective:

The appliance industry /
has been victimized /

by a compression factor /
which resulted /
in an increase /
in units manufactured / /

By the time you get here the monotony has lost you. Where's the action?

"victimize"?
    "compress"?
     "result"?
       "increase"?
         "manufacture"?

The possible actions are all smeared together. But onward to the rest:

(units were also /
being continuously upgraded /
with options /
as standard equipment) /

The new vertical perspective reveals something else right away—the parenthesis is too long. And it comes when you are already lost. It causes the last element of the sentence simply to hang in the air, like a red flag at the end of a projecting truck cargo.

MAIN LOAD / coupled *with* /
         ——a negative disproportionate rise /
         ——*in* prices.

OK. We've read this baby aloud and know there is a problem *somewhere*. Where? As always, let's start with the *action*. Can we visualize it?

The **appliance industry** has been **victimized by a compression**

21

factor which resulted in an increase in units manufactured (units were also being continuously upgraded with options as standard equipment) coupled with a negative disproportionate rise in prices.

If you are "victimized by a compression factor" what's happening to you? *You are being "squeezed."* So we have a subject and a verb:

The appliance industry is being squeezed.

Next, we might logically ask, "squeezed *between what and what?*"

The appliance industry has been victimized by a compression factor which resulted in **an increase in units manufactured** (units were also being continuously upgraded with options as standard equipment) coupled with **a negative disproportionate rise in prices.**

This unweeded garden of a sentence contains the answer if we search for it.

1. On one side **an increase in units manufactured.** Aha! An old friend from Econ 10 called *oversupply.*
2. On the other, pulling the blanket off **a negative disproportionate rise in prices** reveals another Econ 10 acquaintance—*higher prices!*

OK, how do we create a shape that reflects this compression? Is this really a biggie? Why not just:

The appliance industry **is being squeezed** between oversupply and rising prices.

The parenthetical qualification really doesn't fit in the sentence. Only one solution—leave it out. Every utterance poses a trade-off dilemma between specificity and emphasis. Go for the emphasis. If you must have the detail, write another sentence, itself emphatic. So here, put the parenthetical element, if really needed, in a second sentence.

My revision may, though, be misconstruing the sentence. Look at the first part again.

> The appliance industry has been victimized by a compression factor which resulted in an increase in units manufactured . . .

As written, the "compression factor" *causes* the increase in "units manufactured." Again, stylistic interference makes the writer *misconstrue the central causality* of the process. This is a **big** mistake.

And so, original and revision:

Original

> The appliance industry has been victimized by a compression factor which resulted in an increase in units manufactured (units were also being continuously upgraded with options as standard equipment) coupled with a negative disproportionate rise in prices. (37 words)

Revision

> The appliance industry is being squeezed between oversupply and rising prices. (11 words; LF 70%)

So we can add three more rules to the Paramedic Method, to help us revise for a shape which reflects meaning.

1. Circle the prepositions.
2. Circle the "is" forms.
3. Ask, "Where's the action?" "Who's kicking who?"
4. Put this "kicking" action in a simple (not compound) active verb.
5. Start fast—no slow windups.

6. Write out each sentence on a blank sheet of paper and mark off its basic rhythmic units with a " / ".
7. Read the passage aloud with emphasis and feeling.
8. Mark off sentence lengths in the passage with a " / ".

PM Super Slim and the "Real You" Sentence

Sometimes you can *see* a natural sentence shape trying to emerge through the lard:

All that it really means is that more and more software will be developed faster and faster and that the software will be much more reliable and easier to maintain.

Here's a basic shape fighting for life:

more and more
faster and faster

more reliable
easier to maintain.

"More and more," "faster and faster," and "easier." You always want to *build on* patterns such as this; give the eye and ear a chance to reinforce the meaning. Revision here is dead easy.

All that it really means is that more and more software will be developed faster and faster and **that the software** will be much more reliable and easier to maintain.

The slo-mo "Blah blah *is that*" opening gets snipped onto the cutting-room floor, as does "that the software," yielding

More and more software will be developed faster and faster, and will be more reliable and easier to maintain.

The sentence has lost a few pounds (19 instead of 30 words; LF 37%) but the great improvement lies in its *shape*: nicer to look at, quicker to understand, easier to remember.

Shapeless prose has a hard time conveying strong feeling, or emphasizing its point. The emotional power in its water-logged sentences simply seeps away. So the following confession of an advertising person:

> Financial influence of commercial sponsors have [*sic*] devalued the quality of prime time television. Educational and social value of the programs are of secondary importance, as long as the producers can achieve the ratings expected by broadcasters and sponsors.

First a revision and then its rationale:

> Commercial sponsors have ruined prime time television. They have sacrificed educational and social values to audience ratings.

First, I tried to find the *primary actor* in this drama—the "commercial sponsors," rather than their derivative, "financial influence."

Second, I made this primary actor the subject in both sentences, to give them a parallel structure that you can see and hear:

> Commercial sponsors . . .
>
> They . . .

Third, I have used two strong active verbs, "ruined" and "sacrificed."

The action in the sentence is strong, but the verbs the writer has chosen—"devalued" and "are of secondary importance"—generate no force. And the amount of sheer lard in the original sentence makes things even worse. Again, original and revision:

> Financial influence of commercial sponsors have [*sic*] devalued the quality of prime time television. Educational and social value of the programs are of secondary importance, as long as the producers can achieve the ratings expected by broadcasters and sponsors. (38 words)

> Commercial sponsors have ruined prime time television. They have sacrificed educational and social values to audience ratings. (17 words; LF 63%)

Punchless prose such as this projects a flabby, muddle-headed public self, the last thing a businessperson wants to do. Don't demonstrate in public that your mind needs six months at the local gym. With such a caution in hand, look at this piece of everyday business prose:

> On the basis of the answers to these and other questions which the team might ask, I would expect the team to present us with detailed recommendations for enhancing the effectiveness of our reporting. If the recommendations are approved, we would begin to implement them immediately upon completion of the project. I would welcome a team with a broad diversity of interests, including but not limited to human resource management. Because of the focus on reporting, I would especially welcome the participation of at least one individual with a strong interest in Finance or Accounting.

Nothing really serious here, no arm numbness or deep chest pain. Just flab, flab, flab, and its accompanying arrhythmia. Needless repetition: "the team . . . the team." Strings of jaw-breaking tongue twisters: "recommendations for enhancing the effectiveness." A kind of flamenco chorus of aye, aye, ayes: "I would expect . . . I would welcome . . . I would especially welcome:" And all so easy to fix:

~~On the basis of the answers to~~ *By answering* (these) ~~and other~~ questions ~~which~~ *like*
the team ~~might ask, I would expect the team to present us with~~ *should be able to*
~~detailed~~ recommend~~ations for enhancing the effectiveness of~~ *improvements in* our
reporting. ~~If~~ *if* the recommendations are approved, ~~we~~ would ~~begin~~ *be*
to implement ~~them~~ immediately ~~upon completion of the project.~~ *want ed*
I ~~would welcome~~ *want* a team with a broad ~~diversity of~~ interests,
~~including but not limited to~~ *especially in* human resource management *and, given* ~~Be-~~
~~cause of~~ the (focus) ~~on~~ reporting, ~~I would especially welcome the~~
~~participation of at least one individual with a strong interest~~ in
Finance or Accounting.

By answering questions like these, the team should be able to recommend improvements in our reporting. The recommendations, if approved, would be implemented immediately. I want a team with broad interests, especially in human resource management and, given the reporting focus, in Finance or Accounting. (94 words to 45; LF 52%)

The great improvement here comes in *voice*: crisper, clearer, faster, more emphatic—a voice in command.

THE LONG MARCH: A LAWYER'S SENTENCE

The masters of shapeless prose are the lawyers. Here is a sentence from a typical loan contract:

In the event Buyer defaults on any payment, or fails to obtain or maintain the insurance required hereunder, or fails to comply with any other provision hereof, or a proceeding in bankruptcy, receivership or insolvency shall be instituted by or against Buyer or his property, or Seller deems the property in danger of misuse or confiscation, or Seller otherwise reasonably deems the indebtedness or the property insecure, Seller shall have the right to declare all amounts due or to become due hereunder to be immediately due and payable.

This sentence confuses the ordinary reader—perhaps its intent—by distending its shape. Between the opening "In the event" and the clause which completes this meaning, "Seller shall have the right . . . " intervene a whole string of qualifications.

> In the event **Buyer defaults** on any payment, or fails to obtain or maintain the insurance required hereunder, or fails to comply with any other provision hereof, or a proceeding in bankruptcy, receivership or insolvency shall be instituted by or against Buyer or his property, or Seller deems the property in danger of misuse or confiscation, or Seller otherwise reasonably deems the indebtedness or the property insecure, **Seller shall have the right** to declare all amounts due or to become due hereunder to be immediately due and payable.

We lose our way because we don't know what the qualifications apply to. The main utterance comes last instead of first, where it would orient us. Here the sentence *shape* is reinforced by the *typography*. The convention of consecutive prose obscures the shape of thought. On an electronic screen, we can now suspend that sometimes confusing convention and reshape for thought. I won't change the wording at all, just the order and the layout:

> Seller shall have the right to declare all amounts due or to become due hereunder to be immediately due and payable, in the event
>
> 1. Buyer defaults on any payment, or fails to obtain or maintain the insurance required hereunder, or
> 2. fails to comply with any other provision hereof, or
> 3. a proceeding in bankruptcy, receivership or insolvency shall be instituted by or against Buyer or his property, or
> 4. Seller deems the property in danger of misuse or confiscation, or

5. Seller otherwise reasonably deems the indebtedness or the property insecure.

Typographical arrangement is not sacred. It was imposed upon us by the technology of lead type and that imposition has now been lifted. In the world of paper and print, white space costs money. On a screen, it's free. We can use this new power of the electronic word as a fundamental tool of analysis and reshaping. Nothing easier, as with this simple transformation of a routine legal sentence, one which confronts many consumers.

Now let me carry the transformation one step further, revising out the formulaic repetition and enhancing the argument typographically.

Seller can declare all amounts immediately payable, if

1. **Buyer** defaults on payment or insurance
2. **Buyer** fails to comply with any other provision
3. **Buyer** goes bankrupt
4. **Seller** deems the indebtedness or property in danger

Whether or not the *writer* uses such a presentation, the *reader* can now recreate it as necessary. Anybody interested in revising prose should use this formatting weapon to the full.

Since I'm not an attorney, I don't know how my revision would stand at law. I have simply revised for *shape*, removing the formulaic repetition and using typography to help me understand what is being written. Happily, we have a check on my revision. I took this example from an article on plain-language laws ("Plain-Language Laws: Giving the Consumer an Even Break," Michael Ferry and Richard B. Teitelman, *Clearinghouse Review*, Vol. 14, No. 6 [Oct. 1980, pp. 522ff.]). The authors give a legally sound translation, but one which I have not reviewed since I first read the article several years ago. I'll turn the page now and see what their revision looks like:

We can declare the full amount you owe us due any time we want to.

Ah! They have been more daring than I dared to be—but then, they are lawyers. They have a right to be. But even if we had been willing to desert the law library for the world of common sense, as they did, going through the revision we practiced would be the best way to do it. When you are revising, always proceed step by step. If you just junk the sentence and substitute a paraphrase of your own, even though—as here—that may finally be the best thing to do, you'll not learn *why* the prose defeated you. Here, shape, shape, shape.

CLOSE FOCUS

Shaping a sentence, then, means focusing an idea. Look at the following shapeless blur:

> We are not anxious to casually spend the company's money but our recommendation is intended to minimize the risk involved in launching a new product and a new category into an environment where there exists a vacuum of current knowledge and interest from both consumer and retailer.

Here the chick struggling out of the egg is named *Contrast*: a bad way to spend the company's money (needless research) versus a good way to spend the company's money (research that launches a product with minimum risk). The sentence as written smears this contrast over five lines. Neither eye nor ear lends the mind any help. How do we get these two powerful allies on our side? How about this:

> We don't want to waste the company's money on needless research, but informative research can save money in launching a new product, especially in an unknown market.

1. We've set up an "X" pattern that brings the contrast to quick visual focus.

2. You put contrasted ideas in similar phrases ("waste money" and "save money," "needless research" and "informative research").
3. You invert the basic order in the second element— "money . . . research" becomes "research . . . money" to show that you have inverted the cash flow.
4. And the new visual shape invites the voice to emphasize the contrast; stress "waste" and "needless" in the first element, "informative" and "save" in the second.
5. A little final guff-removal converts

> into an environment where there exists a vacuum of current knowledge and interest from both consumer and retailer

into

> especially in an unknown market.

Here are the original and the revision again:

Original

We are not anxious to casually spend the company's money but our recommendation is intended to minimize the risk involved in launching a new product and a new category into an environment where there exists a vacuum of current knowledge and interest from both consumer and retailer. (47 words)

Revision

We don't want to waste the company's money on needless research, but informative research can save money in launching a new product, especially in an unknown market. (27 words)

A sentence whose shape helps launch its idea and a lard factor of 43%—a sentence half as long and twice as good. And think of the back pressure: writing prose that *sees* clearly may help us to *think* clearly.

HIDING THE BALL

Sometimes a blurred prose shape comes less from ineptitude than from design. Here is another little shopping baglet trying to hide something:

> As indicated previously, it would be speculative to attempt a prediction of the financial liability of the public airport proprietor in the event it had to bear the financial responsibility for damage under judgments made against it on account of aircraft noise.

The mixture as before:

> As indicated previously,
> it **would be** speculative
>   **to** attempt a prediction
>   *of* the financial liability
>   *of* the public airport proprietor
>   *in* the event it had to bear the financial
>   responsibility
>   *for* damage
>   *under* judgments made against it
>   *on* account
>   *of* aircraft noise.

Financial liability poses a sticky wicket for this writer of an environmental impact statement. The city fathers who want to buy the airport hired him to write the report, and they don't want this appalling liability specter to make the scene. If the writer had been an ordinary citizen and not a hired gun, he or she might have just said, "Nobody has any idea how much money aircraft noise suits could cost the city." But that skillful side-by-side placement of the two parallel central elements— "has any idea" and "how much money"—detonates just the land mine that the writer has been tiptoeing around. Notice how the eye leads the voice to wrap itself around "has any idea," to raise both pitch and stress when you pronounce it? To avoid this, the writer has taken refuge in the full Official Style. Look again:

> As indicated previously, it would be speculative to attempt a prediction of the financial liability of the public airport proprietor in the event it had to bear the financial responsibility for damage under judgments made against it on account of aircraft noise.

The standard Official Style drill:

1. "To be" verb (here "would be") plus a string of prepositional phrases.
2. Kicker evaporated out of sight in an impersonal construction ("it would be speculative").
3. Real verb, "predict," stuffed safely out of sight down in "to attempt a prediction of."
4. *Really* scary verb ("pay") *really* stuffed out of sight in "bear the financial liability for."

The Official Style stuffs the danger out of sight into a 42-word bag. Our commonsense version—"Nobody has any idea how much money aircraft-noise suits could cost the city"— focuses it in 14 words (LF 66%).

EXIT FOCUS

The awkwardness we've been chronicling, however, sometimes comes less from chicanery than from an exaggerated desire for precision. The authors spell everything out because they are afraid of being fired—or sued—if they don't. People writing government regulations are specially fond of this habit. If we number every streak of the tulip, somehow that will make instantly clear what the tulip is like, focus essence through an enumeration of particulars. So in the following piece of Official Style:

MOTOR VEHICLE SAFETY STANDARD NO. 217

Bus Window Retention and Release
(Docket No. 2–10; Notice 3)
    The standard requires emergency exit location markings to be placed in certain occupant spaces because of a possible contradiction under the proposed standard between the requirement that the identification markings be located within 6 inches of the point of operation and the requirement that the markings be visible to a seated occupant. The NHTSA has concluded that emergency egress could be hindered if the passenger has difficulty in finding the marking, and that location of the marking outside of an occupant space containing an adjacent seat, which could be permitted under the proposed standard, could create this problem. At the same time it is desirable for the identification and instructions to be located near the point of release. Therefore the final rule requires that when a release mechanism is not located within an occupant space containing an adjacent seat, a label indicating the location of the nearest release mechanism shall be placed within the occupant space.

Businesspeople must cope with this kind of prose every day. The usual Official Style problems present themselves: the "is" + prepositional-phrase habit, the shopping-bag shape, and especially the wonderful bureaucratic delight in spelling out the obvious, as in "emergency egress could be hindered if the passenger has difficulty in finding the marking."

But above all it lacks *focus*. We don't know which assertions are central, which are derivative and subordinate. Again, a problem of who's kicking who, but this time on a paragraph as well as on a sentence level. Let's try the Paramedic Method, even if we are not sure what the passage means. No cheap shot intended; writing this kind of detailed instruction is hard. If I've mistaken the meaning in my revision, try one of your own.

Here goes. We are sitting in a bus, trying to decide where to put the emergency exit signs that indicate a pop-out window. Standard No. 217 requires that in addition to the emergency exit signs placed next to the pop-out windows themselves, signs pointing to the exits be placed in rows of seats not next to pop-out windows. Thus everyone not sitting next to an exit window will be directed to one. A good deal of specific detail accompanies this central rule. What we need, then, is a short and emphatic opening sentence that will tell us what we're doing. Notice how badly the opening sentence does this job. Here it is again:

> The standard requires emergency exit location markings to be placed in certain occupant spaces because of a possible contradiction under the proposed standard between the requirement that the identification markings be located within 6 inches of the point of operation and the requirement that the markings be visible to a seated occupant.

Too many things are happening on the same level:

1. Emergency exit location markings have to be placed in "certain occupant spaces," but those spaces are not defined until later.
2. A possible contradiction exists between the two other requirements.
3. Signs 6″ from the window.
4. Signs to be visible to a seated occupant.

Two ways to skin this cat. Either you can start with a causal sequence: "The proposed standard requires both (3) and (4) and they conflict; *therefore*, we propose the following." Or you can start with the new standard itself and then explain how it came to be. Let's try both openings and see which is better.

Revision 1

The proposed standard requires two things:

1. emergency window exit signs must be within 6″ of the window;
2. every seated passenger must be able to see the sign.

These two requirements sometimes conflict. If you are sitting in a row of seats not next to an emergency window, you won't be able to see the sign. Standard 217 requires that these rows have a sign directing you to the emergency window.

Or

Revision 2

Standard 217 requires that seat rows not next to emergency exit windows include signs directing passengers to the exit windows. The present standard includes two provisions that conflict. First, every emergency window exit must be marked by a sign within 6″ of the window. Second, every seated passenger must be able to see the sign. But what about passengers seated in rows not next to an emergency window? They might not be able to see the sign. NHTSA has concluded that signs should be placed in those rows directing passengers to the emergency windows.

These revisions take care of the first paragraph. Word counts for the sentences run this way:

Original: 52-46-20-38
Revision 1: 30-5-23-15
Revision 2: 20-8-16-11-13-9-17

The revisions vary the sentence length more but, more important, they make them all shorter. A very long sentence, to stay in your head all at once, has to have a very clear framework. It may use parallelism, parentheses, contrasts, alliteration, a whole repertoire of patterns. Without these patterns as a guide, the reader soon gets lost. Shorter sentences solve the problem in a different way. In the revisions, the central idea—because two requirements conflict, we need a third—occurs in two different ways but takes a spotlight in both. Which revision is better? The first, probably. Shorter than the second (71 words against 94; LF 54% and 39%), it also uses the short/long focusing strategy better.

The PM revisions have done other things besides vary sentence length, to be sure. The "is" + preposition formula has been broken up, the diction simplified ("location marking" = "sign"), the reader has been reassigned his humanity ("you" for "occupant"), and the sentences given a little shape. As a result of these changes, the passage's central assertion seems a little clearer. Maybe we could revise yet again, using some of that free white screen space.

Revision 3

The proposed Standard 217 requires three things:

1. emergency window exit signs must be within 6″ of the window;
2. seated passengers must be able to see the signs;
3. if they can't see the window signs, post an extra sign they can see.

Radical therapy, this. We've deleted the "possible contradiction" thread of the argument. But look what has been gained: LF 75%; paragraph reduced to one sentence; above all, *focus*. The regulation's essence leaps to the eye. Sentence shape supplies exactly the kind of specificity needed. Each revision represents a trade-off between emphasis and detail. Wouldn't the third be the best bet if you were writing Standard 217?

Logo Odors

As a last example of prose shapelessness, look at this letter from a cosmetics company to a design firm:

> Pheromone Fragrances, Inc. is evaluating its corporate design needs for the near and intermediate term. The purpose of this effort is to determine how the image of the company might be best promoted or modified to assist us in meeting our growth goals. Your firm is one of the eight firms who have either been in contact with us or who have been recommended by our senior advisors as having the requisite talent, skills, and experience to assist us in this effort. Our plan is to conduct a detailed review of all submissions and to select three or four firms to meet with our executive staff and senior advisors to present any additional materials or information they desire. The design services the company employs must be able to make a positive contribution toward this goal in terms of the external image, awareness, and recognition of Pheromone as a leader in its field.

Not bad prose—just boring, lifeless. You notice first the bad match between a cosmetics company, which must be sensitive to style above all, and the stylistic insensitivity of a prose like this. If their products are as lumpen as their prose, no wonder they need a logo doctor. The way a company writes *is* a logo, the most revealing one of all. Prose style always carries this symbolic charge, declares how sensitive, or insensitive, a company is to the whole stylistic dimension of human behavior. Here, a disastrous mismatch.

Notice, for a start, how four of the five sentences use the same verb, *is*—the weakest, most listless, least specific propellant a sentence can use:

> Pheromone Fragrances, Inc. *is* evaluating . . .
> The purpose of this effort *is* to determine . . .
> Your firm *is* one . . .
> Our plan *is* to conduct . . .

Prose like this declares: "We have no imagination! We cannot *see* language! We cannot *hear* it! We are not easily bored! We love formulaic thinking! We like slow openings, take our time getting to the point, and like to say everything at least twice!" That is, "We don't care about first impressions!" In a *cosmetics* company? Impressions, especially first ones, are what cosmetics create. A cosmetics company ought not to write this way, but more important, they ought not to think this way— blind to the stylistic surface of human life. That surface drives their business. No wonder they have an image problem.

Again, so easy to fix. Let's start with the first two sentences:

Pheromone Fragrances, Inc. is evaluating its corporate design needs for the near and intermediate term. The purpose of this effort is to determine how the image of the company might be best promoted or modified to assist us in meeting our growth goals.

You are struck first, in these two sentences, by what we might call an action blur. All kinds of actions are suggested but none are stressed or focused.

evaluating

design

needs

purpose

effort

determine

image

promoted

modified

assist

meeting

growth

A dozen possible actions are first suggested and then dribbled across the sentence. Again, the symbolism grabs you by the lapel: here is a company that does not know what to do first or at all. The sentence models, in the most graphic way possible, a management failure—a failure to think. Instead of thought, it gives us the history—through all those nascent actions—of its failed attempts to think. This constitutes the business equivalent of the student's paper about how hard it is to write a paper.

What action should stand center stage? *Need.* "Pheromone Fragrances, Inc. needs. . . ." All right. What does it need? *To change its image.* Why? *To increase sales.* This sequence should stand center stage:

> To increase sales, Pheromone Fragrances, Inc. needs to improve its image.

Why not just say this? Because it does not sound impressive enough. No one will know the writer has an MBA. And so we add needless specificity—"near and intermediate term." You use two words, "promoted or modified," where one will do. You string prepositional phrases together with infinitives into our standard laundry list. This makes the prose not only shapeless but pompous.

Revising the rest is easy. Original again:

> Your firm is one of the eight firms who have either been in contact with us or who have been recommended by our senior advisors as having the requisite talent, skills, and experience to assist us in this effort. Our plan is to conduct a detailed review of all submissions and to select three or four firms to meet with our executive staff and senior advisors to present any additional materials or information they desire. The design services the company employs must be able to make a positive contribution toward this goal in terms of the external image, awareness, and recognition of Pheromone as a leader in its field.

Let's take it one sentence at a time. For the first, we simply remove needless detail.

Original

Your firm is one of the eight firms who have either been in contact with us or who have been recommended by our senior advisors as having the requisite talent, skills, and experience to assist us in this effort.

Revision

Your firm is one of eight from whom we have requested submissions.

Second sentence:

Original

Our plan is to conduct a detailed review of all submissions and to select three or four firms to meet with our executive staff and senior advisors to present any additional materials or information they desire.

Revision

We will review the submissions and ask three or four firms to meet with our senior staff.

Here we have focused the natural subject ("Our plan is to conduct" = "We will"). We have found the central action and made it the central verb ("conduct a detailed review" = "review"). Instead of spelling out the obvious, we've pared to essentials ("executive staff and senior advisors to present any additional materials or information they desire" = "to meet with our senior staff").

Third sentence:

Original

The design services the company employs must be able to make a positive contribution toward this goal in terms of the external image, awareness, and recognition of Pheromone as a leader in its field.

Revision

The design service finally selected must show Pheromone how to present itself as a leader in its field.

Action! Action! Action!
Contribute becomes "be able to make a positive contribution toward." See how this circumlocution smears the action across eight words when you need only one?

And what does "in terms of" really mean? How does it relate to "external image"?

And what other kinds of image besides "external" can be meant here anyway?

And who is aware of what in "awareness"? Who is recognizing whom? When a businessperson loses track of who is doing what to whom, he or she is in deep marmalade. Who is kicking who? Here, all the actions are so vague and smeared you don't know what is going on or who is where. This muddled action is not a trifling matter. It points directly to the muddled thought that makes Pheromone need to spend a lot of money perking up its image.

Here is the original again. Read it aloud and without hurry:

Pheromone Fragrances, Inc. is evaluating its corporate design needs for the near and intermediate term. The purpose of this effort is to determine how the image of the company might be best promoted or modified to assist us in meeting our growth goals. Your firm is one of the eight firms who have either been in contact with us or who have been recommended by our senior advisors as having the requisite talent, skills, and experience to assist us in this effort. Our plan is to conduct a detailed review of all submissions and to select three or four firms to meet with our executive staff and senior advisors to present any additional materials or information they desire. The design services the company employs must be able to make a positive contribution toward this goal in terms of the external image, awareness, and recognition of Pheromone as a leader in its field. (152 words)

Here is the revision:

To increase sales, Pheromone Fragrances, Inc. needs to improve its corporate image. Your firm is one of eight from whom we have received design proposals. We will review the proposals and ask three or four firms to meet with our senior staff before we make a final choice. (48 words; LF 68%)

Business folk like to think themselves blunt bottom-liners, but they very seldom write that way. If this plain opening seems too blunt or bald, ask yourself why. Is it the kind of need a company should be embarrassed about? Or pompous about, to cover over the embarrassment? We have cut the passage by two thirds. *Farewell* the blurred action, the pomposity, the sheer mindless guff. *Welcome* the two-thirds savings in writing materials, writing time, and writing thought. We have given the sentences a shape which reflects their meaning. Have we sacrificed a ceremonial courtesy, or a euphemistic delicacy about final purpose, in doing so? I think not, but it would be fun to argue the other side. Try an alternative revision with that in mind.

CHAPTER 3

VOICE, RHYTHM, SOUND, SENTENCE LENGTH

Voice, rhythm, sound—too much like poetry? Here's a typical piece of the prose which businesspeople absorb every day:

> Malodorous emissions at airports are largely due to unburned aromatics and partially oxidized fuel components such as organic acids. Thus, malodorous emissions are largely due to aircraft operations. Airport vehicular traffic and jet fuel vapor also contribute to the olfactory impact. The hydrocarbon concentration presented in Figures II-11, II-12, and II-13 can be considered as a measure of products of incomplete combustion, since they are the major odor source. Based upon this comparison, it would appear that those areas in the immediate vicinity of the runways and terminal areas would be most impacted by the malodors.

Let's start off by applying rule 8: Mark off sentence lengths in the passage with a " / ":

1. Malodorous emissions at airports are largely due to unburned aromatics and partially oxidized fuel components such as organic acids. (19 words)
2. Thus, malodorous emissions are largely due to aircraft operations. (9 words)
3. Airport vehicular traffic and jet fuel vapor also contribute to the olfactory impact. (13 words)
4. The hydrocarbon concentration presented in Figures II-11, II-12, and II-13 can be considered as a measure of products of incomplete combustion, since they are the major odor source. (28 words)
5. Based upon this comparison, it would appear that those areas in the immediate vicinity of the runways and terminal areas would be most impacted by the malodors. (27 words)

Too many long sentences. There's a place to start. There is some variety in length (19–9–13–28–27) from sentence to sentence that could create dramatic interest, but the opportunity for emphasis is thrown away. We'll wade in, as usual, sentence by sentence:

Original

Malodorous emissions at airports are largely due to unburned aromatics and partially oxidized fuel components such as organic acids. (19 words)

Revision

Airport odors are usually caused by unburned fuel: aromatics, organic acids, and the like. (14 words; LF 26%)

Query: Instead of *odors*, how about *smells* or even *stinks?*

2. Original

Thus, malodorous emissions are largely due to aircraft operations. (9 words)

3. Original

Airport vehicular traffic and jet fuel vapor also contribute to the olfactory impact. (13 words)

Revision (of 2 and 3)

Airport odors are usually caused by airplanes and cars. (9 words; LF 59%)

4. Original

The hydrocarbon concentration presented in Figures II-11, II-12, and II-13 can be considered as a measure of products of incomplete combustion, since they are the major odor source. (28 words)

Revision

The major hydrocarbon concentration presented in Figures II-11, II-12, and II-13 represents incomplete combustion. (14 words; LF 50%)

5. Original

Based upon this comparison, it would appear that those areas in the immediate vicinity of the runways and terminal areas would be most impacted by the malodors. (27 words)

Revision

Since the worst smells come from the airplanes, the areas closest to them smell the worst. (16 words; LF 37%)

I've reduced and varied sentence length somewhat:

Original: 19-9-13-28-27
Revision: 14-9-14-16

But it's not a terrific improvement. Maybe I can cut the Gordian knot in a final revision:

Original

Malodorous emissions at airports are largely due to unburned aromatics and partially oxidized fuel components such as organic acids. Thus, malodorous emissions are largely due to aircraft operations. Airport vehicular traffic and jet fuel vapor also contribute to the olfactory impact. The hydrocarbon concentration presented in Figures II-11, II-12, and II-13 can be considered as a measure of products of incomplete combustion, since they are the major odor source. Based upon this comparison, it would appear that those areas in the immediate vicinity of the runways and terminal areas would be most impacted by the malodors. (96 words)

Revision

Because unburned aircraft fuel (aromatics, organic acids, and the like) causes most airport smells, the areas closest to aircraft smell the worst. (22 words; LF 77%)

Well, I've skunked myself. So much for varying sentence length. I wanted so much to break the monotony that I ended up with a single sentence. If you can revise your passage into a single sentence, of course, you don't need to worry about relative sentence length. I have cut out some detail to focus the *cause-and-effect* relationship. Put the detail, if you really need it, in a couple of short sentences to follow.

CHARTING

Word processors provide a simple yet useful procedure for measuring sentence length. Put each sentence into a separate paragraph and see what it looks like. Then do a word count for each and put the totals in the right margin. Or, if you are working on paper, take a piece of your prose and a red pencil and draw a slash after every sentence. Two or three pages ought to make a large enough sample. If the red marks occur at regular intervals, you have, as they used to say in the White House, a problem. You can chart the problem another way, if you like. Choose a standard length for one sentence and then do a bar graph. Nothing to it on an electronic screen. If it looks like this:

   _____

   _____

   _____

   _____

   _____

   _____

   _____

peachy. If like this:

   _____

   _____

   _____

   _____

   _____

not so peachy.

Obviously, no absolute quantitative standards exist for how much variety is good, how little bad, but the principle couldn't be easier. Vary sentence length. Naturally enough, complex patterns will fall into long sentences, and emphatic conclusions work well when short. But no general rule prevails except to avoid monotony. When you think about sentence length in a *particular* case, of course, all the other concomitant variables of style enter in since they determine sentence length to begin with. You can't revise a passage only to vary sentence length. In fact, a varied pattern usually reflects other stylistic choices already made; rather than constituting an end in itself, it represents a relative virtue, an appearance of health rather than a vital sign. But it does provide an easy place to begin voicing your prose, giving it a recognizable and forceful human personality.

Again, the PM:

1. Circle the prepositions.
2. Circle the "is" forms.
3. Ask, "Where's the action?" "Who's kicking who?"
4. Put this "kicking" action in a simple (not compound) active verb.
5. Start fast—no slow windups.
6. Write out each sentence on a blank sheet of paper and mark off its basic rhythmic units with a " / ".
7. Read the passage aloud with emphasis and feeling.
8. Mark off sentence lengths in the passage with a " / ".

Let's try now exercising rule 8 on the following passage:

Original

It is important to bring forth the problems and other obstacles that are hindering our performance and growth. To be successful we must grow and to grow we must identify our problems and deal with them. Time will be allowed for discussions after each presentation to focus on the problems and potential solutions.

Sentence length:

It is important to bring forth the problems and other obstacles that are hindering our performance and growth. (18 words)

To be successful we must grow and to grow we must identify our problems and deal with them. (18 words)

Time will be allowed for discussions after each presentation to focus on the problems and potential solutions. (17 words)

The gods are against us.

_____ (18 words)
_____ (18 words)
_____ (17 words)

Again, this kind of external measurement does not provide an infallible rule. It offers only a way into sentence voicing, an external indication of internal problems. Here, there is no voice, only a bland impersonality. Let's see what happens to voice when we try to break up that monotonous sentence length problem:

Original

It is important to bring forth the problems and other obstacles that are hindering our performance and growth.

Revision

What problems hinder our performance and growth?

1. A 61% Lard Factor.
2. No more dead-rocket opening ("It is important to bring forth . . .").
3. No more needless repetition ("problems and other obstacles").
4. A seven-word sentence to break up the 18–18–17 pattern.
5. But above all a definite and direct voice.

With a seven-word sentence preceding, we can leave the second one pretty much as is:

To be successful we must grow and to grow we must identify our problems and deal with them.

To succeed we must grow and to grow we must identify—and deal with—our problems.

We need only change "to be" plus an adjective ("successful") to the simple and much stronger infinitive ("to succeed"). Notice how this change strengthens the natural power of the AB : BC pattern of "To succeed—grow; to grow—identify."

51

The voice in this sentence comes across clearly; furthermore, it gains power from the clear voicing of the previous sentence. Thus a prose personality takes life.

Original

Time will be allowed for discussions after each presentation to focus on the problems and potential solutions.

Revision

After each presentation, we will discuss problems and possible solutions.

We have followed rule 3 of the PM, found the actor ("we"), and given ourselves (rule 4) a simple active verb ("discuss"). We have followed rule 5, too; we have started faster and gotten much sooner to the "discuss problems" heart of the sentence. If we follow rule 7, read the sentence aloud with emphasis and feeling, it sounds pretty good. Try it. The triple "p" pattern of "presentation," "problems," and "possible" adds an alliterative smoothness that doesn't obtrude. Sound works with sense.

Now the original again and the revision:

Original

It is important to bring forth the problems and other obstacles that are hindering our performance and growth.

To be successful we must grow and to grow we must identify our problems and deal with them.

Time will be allowed for discussions after each presentation to focus on the problems and potential solutions.

Revision

What problems hinder our performance and growth?

> To succeed we must grow and to grow we must identify—and deal with—these problems.

> After each presentation, we will discuss both problems and possible solutions.

I've tinkered a little further with the revision here. You almost always have to revise for continuity when you reunite sentences revised separately. The bar graph now looks like this:

_____ (7 words)
_____ (16 words)
_____ (11 words)

We have a more varied pattern, and the voice and emphasis that usually come with it.

HOW LONG, O LORD, HOW LONG?

If we can hazard one generalization about sentence length in business writing, it must be this: sentences are almost always too long. A general spirit of dieselizing pervades the office; the engine wants to run on long after you have turned off the key of content. Usually it is a snap to fix.

Original

In developing software, we had to begin from scratch; that is, we were unable to build on previously developed programs.

Revision

In developing software, we had to begin from scratch.

Half as long, twice as strong.
When all the sentences go on too long, the prose swamps

the reader. Look at the following typical example from the wonderful world of data processing:

> Another characteristic of the traditional life cycle is that there is a clear single-string path identified to the user and to Dp from the original feasibility study out through to the implementation of the system. / Finally, a characteristic that renders the system development life cycle unpopular with programmers is the fact that it forces heavy documentation at all stages. / Therefore, some of the perceived disadvantages of systems development life cycle methods are that they can be cumbersome and are sometimes thought to slow down the project. / Additionally, technicians may complain that such rigidity is stifling their creativity. / Finally, the result of the use of all these new techniques and methods is that the user and Dp functions are becoming merged and the Dp development group is being regarded as a service area to the user and in many organizations is being made part of the user group. / The important fundamental to remember is that, even with this apparently dramatic reduction in the length of the system's development life cycle, the basic needs of the original seven stages must still be met, however "hidden" these stages may be. /

The bar graph looks like this:

_____ (35 words)
_____ (24 words)
_____ (27 words)
_____ (11 words)
_____ (50 words)
_____ (40 words)

But the variety here is lost because almost all the sentences go on so long. You crave a quick three- or four-word exclamation. Something with a little zip and emphasis. Let's try putting the PM to work on it. As always, sentence by sentence. (I confess to a severe handicap here—I don't know what the passage means. Since, however, we often have to revise what we cannot fully understand, let's give it a try.)

Original

Another characteristic of the traditional life cycle is that there is a clear single-string path identified to the user and to Dp from the original feasibility study out through to the implementation of the system. (35 words)

Revision

In traditional life cycles, a single-string path clear to user and Dp runs from feasibility study to implementation. (18 words)

Original

Finally, a characteristic that renders the system development life cycle unpopular with programmers is the fact that it forces heavy documentation at all stages. (24 words)

Revision

Programmers dislike this cycle because it requires heavy documentation. (9 words)

Original

Therefore, some of the perceived disadvantages of systems development life cycle methods are that they can be cumbersome and are sometimes thought to slow down the project. (27 words)

Revision

Life cycle methods can be cumbersome and delay the project. (10 words)

Original

Additionally, technicians may complain that such rigidity is stifling their creativity. (11 words)

Revision

And stifle the technicians' creativity. (5 words)

Original

Finally, the result of the use of all these new techniques and
methods is that the user and Dp functions are becoming merged
and the Dp development group is being regarded as a service
area to the user and in many organizations is being made part
of the user group. (50 words)

Revision

Because these new methods merge user and Dp functions, in
many companies the Dp group becomes part of the user group.
(21 words)

Original

The important fundamental to remember is that, even with this
apparently dramatic reduction in the length of the system's development life cycle, the basic needs of the original seven stages
must still be met, however "hidden" these stages may be. (40
words)

Revision

Remember, however, that even with this dramatic reduction in
life cycle development time, the seven original stages must still
be fulfilled. ["processed"? "observed"?] (21 words)

The comparative sentence lengths for original and revision
look like this:

Original: 35-24-27-11-50-40
Revision: 18-9-10-5-21-21

Well, not so bad. We have at least reduced absolute lengths. And varied length somewhat from sentence to sentence. Now let's put the individual revisions back together and see what we have:

Original

Another characteristic of the traditional life cycle is that there is a clear single-string path identified to the user and to Dp from the original feasibility study out through to the implementation of the system. Finally, a characteristic that renders the system development life cycle unpopular with programmers is the fact that it forces heavy documentation at all stages. Therefore, some of the perceived disadvantages of systems development life cycle methods are that they can be cumbersome and are sometimes thought to slow down the project. Additionally, technicians may complain that such rigidity is stifling their creativity. Finally, the result of the use of all these new techniques and methods is that the user and Dp functions are becoming merged and the Dp development group is being regarded as a service area to the user and in many organizations is being made part of the user group. The important fundamental to remember is that, even with this apparently dramatic reduction in the length of the system's development life cycle, the basic needs of the original seven stages must still be met, however "hidden" these stages may be. (187 words)

Revision

In traditional life cycles, a single-string path clear to user and Dp runs from feasibility study to implementation. Programmers dislike this cycle, however, because it requires heavy documentation; life cycle methods can be cumbersome, delay the project, and stifle creativity. Because these new methods merge user and Dp functions, in many companies the Dp group becomes part of the user group. Remember, however, that even with this dramatic reduction in life cycle development time, the seven original stages must still be observed. (82 words; LF 56%)

Again, try reading first original and then revision aloud, with feeling and emphasis. Try an experiment: mark the rise and fall of your voice above each line as you read the two passages. See any patterns? Relation of vocal emphasis and rhythm to sense? If the revision doesn't make you feel better, I've lost my bet.

HOSANNAH!

The credit manager who wrote the following memo avoids all the dangers of the prose swamp we have just waded through:

What can the sales force do to help?

1. Anticipate problems with your accounts. If a credit memo needs to be issued before an invoice can be paid, be sure the proper steps leading to the issuance of the credit memo are taken. Look for and help us remove other "roadblocks" to payment—wrong P.O. numbers, etc.
2. Talk to your customers. Let them know that we appreciate their business and the prompt payment of our invoices. Point out the advantages of a good track record with us.
3. Pounce on your past dues early in the month. Go over those statement sheets we give you. Assist where and how you can. Balances cleared by the 10th will ensure no interruptions of service, untimely "holds," etc.
4. Keep the credit department informed. Fill us in, and help us keep the flow of money and orders going.

What a terrific memo! Not a word wasted! A direct voice that emerges from a vivid series of imperatives: "Anticipate . . . Talk to . . . Let them know . . . Point out . . . Pounce on . . . Go over . . . Keep . . . Fill us in." This natural consequence follows from the basic strategy: an opening imperative, then detailed instructions. Sentence length and rhythm create a clear prose personality here, friendly and cordial but energetic and in control, and expecting you to be as well. You know just where you are, who is kicking who. Every sentence starts fast. The frustrations, and the excitement, of commerce lurk in every line.

The elements of prose style—grammar, syntax, shape, rhythm, emphasis, level of usage, and so on—all work as dependent variables. Change one and you change the rest. But of them all, rhythm constitutes the most vital of prose's life signs. Rhythmless, unemphatic prose always indicates that Tin Ears have taken over.

Cart Tricks and Good Vibes

Here's a passage that struck me as sounding ugly. I wondered why.

> The ICC's definition of local cartage service is that a local cartage carrier is any person who undertakes to transport any class or classes of property by motor vehicle for compensation, when such transportation is performed in interstate or foreign commerce wholly within a municipality or between contiguous municipalities or within a zone adjacent to, and commercially a part of, any such municipality.

Not fair, of course, to ask that such legalistic language be euphonious. But wouldn't it work better if it were? Let me try to enhance some of the sound jingles and clashes typographically. First the "k" sounds.

> The ICC's definition of lo*cal car*tage service is that a lo*cal car*tage *car*rier is any person who underta*kes* to transport any *cl*ass or *cl*asses of property by motor vehi*cle* for *com*pensation . . .

And the "p" and "t" stops:

> The ICC's definition of local car*t*age service is tha*t* a local car*t*age

carrier is any person who undertakes to transport any class or classes of property by motor vehicle for compensation, when such transportation is performed in interstate or foreign commerce wholly within a municipality or between contiguous municipalities or within a zone adjacent to, and commercially a part of, any such municipality.

And the "–tion" *shun* words: definition, transportation, compensation.

It may not be a statistical anomaly, but isn't it *ugly?* Cacophonous? What to do?

Revision

The ICC defines a local cartage carrier as anyone who transports goods by motor vehicle for pay, when such transportation is performed in interstate or foreign commerce within a municipality or between adjoining ones. (63 words to 34; LF 46%)

Ugly-sounding prose makes you turn off your ears, and when you do that, you shut down a major parameter of prose expressivity. Nobody who wants to be heard can afford to do it.

Squeezing the lard out of prose sometimes liberates a natural rhythm, modest but clear, waiting to be freed. Look at this before-and-after nugget of business reporting:

Before

Whereas the President emerges more as a victor, the Chairman seems defeated.

After

The President seems to win, the Chairman to lose.

A Lard Factor of 25%: the extra words obscure the natural modest stress on "wins" and "loses." Often rhythmic emphasis, once we are sensitive to it, will tell us what to pare away.

SOCIAL DISTANCE

So, too, will the level of formality we strive for. Businesspeople don't usually wear stuffed shirts to work. An easy first-name informality seems far more common. Yet when someone starts to write, what comes out often sounds more like a royal proclamation than a simple exchange of information. Americans have always had trouble with public formality of any sort, from dress to architecture. Maybe that fuels our fondness for the formulas of The Official Style; once we learn them, we can just pour our information into them and forget it. But whatever the reason, colloquial directness occurs rarely in business writing. When a sales manager introduces his colleagues to a new product with "Our baby needs a new name," he illustrates informality at its most efficient—and rarest. So too the sales rep who begins his monthly report with "Wow! What a month!" And this expression of not entirely good-humored vexation projects the same conversational power:

> Well, Jack, another C-303 Program Review has come and gone without advising ABC Control. Contrary to popular belief, we are interested in supporting program management, but we can't do it if we are not part of the team.

This memo needs nothing but praise. The writer seeks to convey not only a fact—once again his office has not been consulted about a review—but his attitude toward that failure and how it affects company welfare. A polite expression of legitimate vexation and anger sometimes works wonders. When you try to do it in The Official Style, though, you often sound stilted and silly:

Dear Roy:

> The purpose of this letter is to make you formally aware of a maintenance situation that has become grossly intolerable and

thus requires immediate remedial action by Derivative Digital Devices (DDD). Since April 2, 1984, DDD field maintenance personnel and Quirky Printer personnel have attempted to fix our system printer, model number 0897. (Attached is a list of available service record receipt numbers.) We are rapidly approaching the four-month mark and our printer is still performing below reasonable, acceptable standards. What is probably untypical is the amount of patience and cooperation I've shown in waiting for DDD field maintenance to resolve this problem. I can no longer wait and therefore urgently request that you motivate at DDD whatever level of authority is required to correct this situation immediately in a manner that is fully acceptable to Anodyne Corp.

Should this letter prove ineffectual in obtaining results, I shall assume that you have abdicated your responsibilities and that I am left to my own resources in dealing with DDD management.

You can see why the writer fell into this style; he wanted the minatory force of a legalistic-sounding warning. But the subject just cries out for the opposite strategy, for a "Look, Jack, if you don't fix this bleeping printer, I'm going to come on over to DDD and start knocking on doors, and when I'm finished you'll wish you'd never been born." At the least, the writer ought to have drawn closer to a conversational tone.

NOT: "What is probably untypical is the amount of patience and cooperation I've shown in waiting for DDD field maintenance to resolve this problem."

INSTEAD: "I've shown the patience of Job in waiting for your people to fix this problem."

NOT: "I can no longer wait and therefore urgently request that you motivate at DDD whatever level of authority is required to

correct this situation immediately in a manner that is fully acceptable to Anodyne Corp."

INSTEAD: "I can't wait any longer. Find somebody—I don't
care at what level—who can fix this printer."

Impatience at incompetence is often justifiable in the business world. It can be expressed through a cold and detached
legalistic prose, but conversational directness often works
better.

Compare the voice, the sense of human personality, behind
the written utterance in the two following passages about pay
and promotion.

Review of the Compensation Structure for Engineers reveals we
are appropriately competitive to retain present good Engineers
and to successfully attract new talent from the labor market. The
weakest point in our wage structure is to competitively compen-
sate new Engineers after they are two or three years into their
experience spectrum. This problem results from the need to give
these Engineers merit increases that better the annual inflation
rate to keep them ahead of the starting salaries of new college
graduates.

How do we stimulate and reward high performance when promotions will be scarce and competition for them fierce?

The second paragraph has a simple, direct, natural voice.
The first one cries out for the PM treatment. Circle the prepositions and infinitives (split or whole) and the "is" forms. Try
to find the action. Do a bar graph of sentence length and then
try to give the sentences some kind of shape and rhythm
related to the human voice.

_____ (27 words)
_____ (24 words)
_____ (30 words)

Too much of a length and too long. How about something like this:

Revision

We pay our engineers competitive beginning salaries. After a couple of years, though, their salaries tend to fall behind those of new college graduates. How do we give them merit increases that stay ahead both of inflation and the beginning salaries of people who have been hired later?

The bar graph looks a little better in the revision:

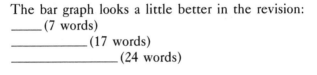

_____ (7 words)
_____ (17 words)
_____ (24 words)

My revision may not be a world-beater, but at least it breaks up the monotony of the passage and moves it several steps toward the crisp conversational voice that makes the second passage good prose. Prose rhythm, then, does not simply paint a gloss over meaning but helps constitute it. Often the rhythm will say as much as the "meaning."
So in this brief example:

The month of April has been spent, for the most part, in assessment of problems and possible solutions, settling priorities, and building and orienting the Task Force. Therefore, most of the accomplishments, although real, are intangible.

The hesitant, broken, back-and-forth rhythm projects a disastrous impression of indecisive muddle. "Well, uh, er, we have had only a, uh, month to try to, you know, get the whole Task Force going and even so we've managed, like, to get quite a lot done, really, I mean considering the time we've had." Who knows, they really may have done a terrific job, however "intangible." But the prose makes it sound just the opposite. It says one thing in matter, another in manner.

THE SOUND OF MUSIC

Sometimes, too, a sentence rhythm will seem worth aiming at just for the sound, for the music of it. Look at how a long string of one-syllable words breaks up the rhythm here:

> The Director's overwhelming presence in relation to that of the rest of the employees strikes us immediately.

Seven one-syllable words in a row dulls the prose bite as well as a string of jawbreakers does. Again, the villain is that string of prepositional phrases. The fix simply lines up kicker and kickee:

> The Director, obviously, overwhelms the other employees.

(Do you see the similarity, within the sentence, to the problem of varying length from sentence to sentence?) Once your ears have had their consciousness raised, they'll catch the easy sound problems as they flow from the pen—"however clever" will become "however shrewd" in the first draft—and the harder ones will seem easier to revise.

Let's try one last revision, massaging a passage that shows just how The Official Style works against a voiced prose, against rhythm, shape, and personality in the sentence. I'll put this whole definition of a Program Manager before you, and then we'll dissect it:

> With regard to your request concerning Program Management and specifically the definition and function of a Program Manager, the following is submitted:
>
> > A Program Manager reports to the General Manager and is a member of his staff.
> >
> > A Program Manager's authority is that of a Director but may be authorized with more authority as designated by the General Manager.

The specific assignment of a Program Manager is to administer a program in its entirety.

The planning function of the program is a responsibility of the Program Manager.

Coordination with the Operating Departments is a necessary activity that the Program Manager must maintain. This coordination effort requires that the functional areas involved be kept aware of what is being enforced so as not to allow this condition to become habitual.

The Program Manager may develop alternative methods of achieving the program goals within accepted organizational parameters. This option is based on the personality of the Program Manager and the nature of the program. This option is limited to the organizational procedures and should not drift far from the norm but should allow for flexibility.

Wallboard prose. The same homogeneous Official Style from beginning to end, cut up by a circular saw into arbitrary sentences. The writer assembles his sentences strictly according to The Official Style formula—"is" plus prepositional-phrase strings:

A Program Manager's authority
  is that
  of a Director but may be authorized
  with more authority
  as designated
  by the General Manager.

The planning function
  of the program
  is a responsibility
  of the Program Manager.

This option
  is based
  on the personality

of the Program Manager
and the nature
of the program.

The actor is hidden in a godlike impersonal construction: "the following is submitted." The sentences use the slow wind-up, "The blah-blah of the blah-blah *is that*," opening formula. And what about sentence length?

_____ (22 words)
_____ (15 words)
_____ (22 words)
_____ (15 words)
_____ (13 words)
_____ (15 words)
_____ (27 words)
_____ (16 words)
_____ (17 words)
_____ (21 words)

Not much variation and all long; standard wallboard sizes. The phrases too come in standard wallboard sizes; tedium itself. But it is when you try applying rule 7 of the PM—reading the passage aloud with feeling and emphasis—that the pompous emptiness of its tautological pronouncements really comes across. Try it.

INTERLOCKING VARIABLES

We can see, in a passage like this, how all the variables of The Official Style interlock. The lifeless, verbless impersonality leads to the "is" plus prepositional-phrase strings which, in turn, lead to the monotonous sentence lengths and phrase lengths, which, in their turn, prohibit any sentence rhythm, and this leads in its turn to voiceless prose, dehumanized and dead. All these attributes constitute everything that good business prose ought not to be. When we try to revise a passage like this, it literally comes apart in our hands, falls into its constituent pieces, and reveals the striking vacuity of its thought. We'll need a sentence-by-sentence revision to see this:

Original

With regard to your request concerning Program Management and specifically the definition and function of a Program Manager, the following is submitted:

Revision

You ask for a job description of Program Manager:

Original

A Program Manager reports to the General Manager and is a member of his staff.

Revision

A Program Manager reports to the General Manager and is on his staff.

Original

A Program Manager's authority is that of a Director but may be authorized with more authority as designated by the General Manager.

Revision

A Program Manager ranks as a Director, but may be given more authority by the General Manager. [I am trying to escape the "*authority* . . . *authorized* with more *authority*" tautological repetition here.]

Original

The specific assignment of a Program Manager is to administer a program in its entirety. The planning function of the program is a responsibility of the Program Manager.

Revision

A Program Manager plans and administers a program.

Maybe we don't need to do the whole thing after all. The last revision, with its Lard Factor of 75%, shows the central vice of the whole passage—empty tautology, a definition that repeats the same word (e.g., "authority") without defining it. The thinking becomes so general and vague that finally the writer starts using words (e.g., "this condition" in the penultimate paragraph) that refer to nothing at all.

Job descriptions are written for people and ought to sound that way. When you have finished applying the PM to a passage like this, a voice with at least some relation to humankind ought to emerge of its own accord. Let me try a last, slightly impressionistic, revision:

Revision

You ask me to define a Program Manager. A Program Manager plans and administers a program and coordinates it with other departments. Reporting to the General Manager and on his staff, a Program Manager ranks as a Director but may be given additional authority by the General Manager.

I've rearranged things a little and left out over half the original. What I've omitted seems to me pure guff. Do you agree? Even if I have left out some details, the recognizable human voice that enters justifies the omission. In the large organizations that need specific job descriptions like this, details fall as thick as snowflakes in Siberia. The recognizable human voice that will state the pattern beyond the detail, and act on it, lies much thinner on the ground. It's that recognizable and responsible voice we should aim for.

CHAPTER 4

THE OFFICIAL STYLE

Up to now we've concentrated on translating The Official Style into plain English. Now, we focus on the style itself. And, instead of simply condemning it, we'll ask how and why it has come about, how it works in the world.

Students of style have traditionally distinguished three basic levels—high, middle, low. The content of these categories varied somewhat, but usually the high style was a formal and ornamental style for a solemn and ritualized occasion, the low style enshrined the loose and sloppy intercourse of daily life, and the middle style stood somewhere in between. Since World War II, American prose has worked a pronounced variation on this enduring pattern. The low style has pretty much disintegrated into a series of "I-mean-like-you-know" shrugs and spastic tics, where I go, "like," and you go, "you know?" And as we have come to suspect fancy language and formal ceremony as undemocratic, we have come to suspect the high style, too. We think of it as "only rhetoric."

As a substitute for both, we've clasped to our bosoms The

Official Style—a style that is formal without ever pretending to be grand. The Official Style is often stigmatized as bureaucratese or jargon, and it often is both. But it is a genuine style, and one that reflects the genuine bureaucratization of American life. It has its own rules and its own ambitions, and everyone today must grapple with them. The Official Style comes to us in many guises but two main ones: as the language of the learned professions and as the language of bureaucracy, whether in government, business, or the military. The learned professions want above all to sound learned and scientific—disinterested, impersonal, factual. Bureaucracy wants above all to sound official—neutral, formal, authoritative, inevitable. Both ambitions converge on a common set of verbal habits, The Official Style.

The Official Style runs from school days to retirement. As soon as you realize that you live "in a system," whether P.S. 41, the University of California, the Department of Agriculture, General Motors, or the Army Signal Corps, you start developing The Official Style. Used unthinkingly, it provides the quickest tip-off that you have become system-sick and look at life only through the system's eyes. It is a scribal style, ritualized, formulaic, using a special vocabulary to describe a special kind of world, the world of bureaucratic officialdom. And it is, increasingly, the only kind of prose style many Americans ever encounter. It is also, along with the social changes that sponsor it, one of the main reasons for our prose problem. The low style has dissolved, the high style has hardened and dehydrated, and the middle style has simply evaporated. The Official Style threatens to replace all three.

If you can analyze, write, and translate it, maybe you can find your niche in the system—public sector or private—without losing your soul to it. For you may have to write in The Official Style, but you don't have to think in it. If you are the first on the scene after the sports car has missed the curve, climbed the hedge, and ended up on the lawn, you won't ask the driver, as did one policeman, "How, uh, sir, did you achieve this configuration?"

THE OFFICIAL BOA

Sometimes you can see The Official Style seizing its prey like a boa constrictor and gradually squeezing the life out of it. Here's a college student first feeling its grip.

> Twelve-year-old boys like to fight. Consequently, on several occasions I explained to them the negative aspects of fighting. Other responsibilities included keeping them dry (when near the creek or at times of rain), seeing that they bathed, attending to any minor wounds they acquired, and controlling their mischievous behavior. Another responsibility was remaining patient with the children.

The first sentence says simply what it has to say. The second sentence starts to sound like a report. It strives for a needless explicitness ("on several occasions") and it aims for a pseudoscientific neutrality of description ("the negative aspects of fighting"). To remain on the same stylistic level as the first sentence, it ought to read, "So, I often told them to stop." "Other responsibilities included" is the language of a job description. The frantic scramble of summer camp life is being viewed through a personnel form. The prose is scary as well as stilted because life has been reduced to something that will fit in a file cabinet. Only on official forms do small boys "acquire minor wounds" or counselors "attend" them. In life, they cut themselves and you give them a Band-Aid. In life, you keep them out of the creek and out of the rain, instead of "keeping them dry (when near the creek or at times of rain)." And, instead of "controlling their mischievous behavior," you make them behave or even give them a kick in the pants. As for "Another responsibility was remaining patient with the children," that translates into, "I had to keep my temper." If the writer had stayed on the stylistic level he began with, he would have written:

> Twelve-year-old boys like to fight. Often, I had to stop them.

And I had to keep them out of the rain, and the creek, and mischief generally. I had to give out Band-Aids and keep my temper. (LF 35%)

Why didn't he? You don't write The Official Style by nature. It has to be learned. Why did he fall into it here? He was *applying for* something. And you apply for something—in this case, admission to medical school—on a form. And a form requires an official style. The Official Style. It makes what you've done sound important and, still more important than important, Official.

Ever since George Orwell's famous essay "Politics and the English Language" (1946), The Official Style has been interpreted as a vast conspiracy to soften our minds and corrupt our political judgment. Social science jargon has been seen as pure hokum, an attempt to seem more scientific than you are. And the language of Pentagon bureaucrats usually combines the worst of the civil bureaucracy and the military high command. The Orwell conspiracy theory is sometimes true, but not the whole truth. We all want to fit in, to talk the language of the country. This desire is what keeps society glued together. So the impulses that attract us to The Official Style are not always perverse or depraved. Just the opposite. They are the primary social impulses. And so when we analyze The Official Style, we're really talking about how we live now, about our society as well as our prose, about how to survive in the system. What does the prose tell us about the society?

EUPHEMISM AND EVASION

Well, it is a euphemistic society, for a start. It thinks of every town dump as a "sanitary landfill site," every mentally retarded child as "exceptional," every dog catcher as an "animal welfare officer," every pigpen as a "unitary hog-raising facility." Society may have its pains and problems, but language can sugarcoat them. An Official Stylist would never say an area was so polluted that plants obviously couldn't grow there. Instead: "Natural biotic habitats are conspicuously absent from the region."

And it is a society with a voracious press, so that officials often have to say something when they have nothing to say, or nothing they *can* say. So when a State Department spokesman was asked how the conference was going, he did not say "God knows!" but instead:

> I think it is already possible that this particular summit is one that is on the way to a substantial result. There has been evidence of an encouragingly large area of agreement toward a concrete and concerted action program by the various countries represented here—a program that will be concise and meaningful in its nature.

The Official Style society is also a society afraid of taking responsibility. The system acts, not the people within it. If its first rule is "Never call anything by its right name," its second is "Keep your head down. Don't assert anything you'll have to take the blame for. Don't, if you can help it, assert anything at all." Anthony Sampson, in his *Anatomy of Britain*, has culled a few examples of this supercaution from the more courtly British Civil Service version of The Official Style and supplied plain language translations.

> We hope that it is fully appreciated that . . .
> You completely fail to realize that . . .
>
> Greater emphasis should be laid on . . .
> You haven't bothered to notice . . .
>
> We have the impression that insufficient study has been given to . . .
> No one has considered . . .
>
> Our enquiry seemed to provide a welcome opportunity for discussions of problems of this kind . . .

No one had thought of that before . . .

We do not think that there is sufficient awareness . . .
There is ignorance . . .

There has been a tendency in the past to overestimate the possibilities of useful short-term action in public investment . . .
You should look ahead . . .

There should be an improvement in the arrangements to enable
ministers to discharge their collective responsibility.
The cabinet should work together.

The rule is clear. Don't assert anything you can get tagged
with later. It may come back to haunt you. So never write "I
think" or "I did." Keep the verbs passive and impersonal: "It
was concluded that" or "Appropriate action was initiated on
the basis of systematic discussion indicating that." Often, as
with politicians being interviewed on TV, The Official Style
aims deliberately at saying nothing at all, but saying it in the
required way. Or at saying the obvious impressively. The Official Stylist must seem in control of everything but responsible
for nothing. Thus a member of Congress, instead of saying
that the government will listen to consumer complaints, says
that it will "review existing mechanisms of consumer input,
thruput, and output and seek ways of improving these linkages
via consumer consumption channels." The Official Style has
seized upon the computer language of *input, output,* and *inter-
face* as a magical poetic diction, a body of sacred and intrin-
sically beautiful metaphors. Thus a U.S. senator indicted on
bribery charges does not ask the advice of his friends. Instead,
bathing in computer charisma, he is "currently receiving personal and political input from my supporters and friends
throughout the state."

It is often hard to tell with The Official Style how much
is self-conscious put-on and how much is real ineptitude,
genuine system-sickness. Students often suspect that the
length and physical weight of their papers is more important

than what they say, yet it is not only in school that papers are graded thus. Here is a famous Washington lawyer, talking about legal language:

> In these days when every other type of professional report, good or poor, is dressed up in a lovely ringed and colored plastic binder, some people still are prone to judge legal performance quantitatively by verbal volume. Thirty years ago two of us answered a difficult and intricate legal problem by concisely writing: "Gentlemen, after examining the statute in your state, all analogous statutes, and all of the cases, we have concluded that what you want to do is lawful." That client was not happy; he went down to Wall Street, got the same opinion backed by thirty turgid typewritten pages, and felt much more comfortable.

> (Quoted in Joseph C. Guelden, *The Superlawyers* [New York: Weybright and Talley, 1972], p. 306.)

HAMLET AND HOG PRICES

It is not only bureaucrats who find length and obscurity impressive. Here is another example of The Official Style inflating something short and sweet:

> A policy decision inexorably enforced upon a depression-prone individual whose posture in respect to his total psychophysical environment is rendered antagonistic by apprehension or by inner-motivated disinclination for ongoing participation in human existence is the necessity for effectuating a positive selection between two alternative programs of action, namely, (a) the continuance of the above-mentioned existence irrespective of the dislocations, dissatisfactions, and disabilities incurred in such a mode, or (b) the voluntary termination of such existence by self-initiated instrumentality, irrespective in this instance of the undetermined character of the subsequent environment, if any, in which the subject may be positioned as an end result of this irrevocable determination.

This must be a joke. In fact it is, one of the clever variations on common clichés by Richard D. Altick, a literary critic. He uses it in a marvellous book called *A Preface to Critical Reading*, the literary text varied is, of course, Hamlet's "To be or not to be, that is the question." It's fun and instructive to take a short familiar quotation and translate it into The Official Style. Pick something at random from a dictionary of quotations and try it. How about this, from *The Book of Common Prayer?* "Wine that maketh glad the heart of man; and oil to make him a cheerful countenance, and bread to strengthen man's heart." Or Miranda's famous declaration from Shakespeare's *Tempest*, "O brave new world, that hath such people in it." Or Tom Paine's "These are the times that try men's souls."

Now, for contrast, The Official Style from a real social scientist, an economist this time.

> The evidence for the cobweb model lies in the quasi-periodic fluctuations in prices of a number of commodities. The hog cycle is perhaps the best known, but cattle and potatoes have sometimes been cited as others which obey the "theorem." . . . That the observed hog cycles were too long for the cobweb theorem was first observed in 1935 by Coase and Fowler (1935, 1937). The graph of cattle prices given by Ezekiel (1938) as evidence for the cobweb theorem implies an extraordinarily long period of production (5–7 years). The interval between successive peaks for other commodities tends to be longer than three production periods.

In the world of the triumphant MBA, businesspeople, especially, have to process reams of such prose. Fortunately for us, we have a translation of this particular passage by someone who understands it—a distinguished economist (and a wonderful prose stylist) named Donald McCloskey:

> The whole notion of the cobweb is based on the ups and downs of, say, hog prices. But hog prices take much longer to go up and down than it takes to raise hogs. Something is wrong. What

is wrong, I'll venture, is that the irrational theory of how farmers make guesses about the future is mistaken. (LF 34%)

(*The Rhetoric of Economics* [Madison: U. of Wisconsin P., 1985], p. 95.)

McCloskey has cut the passage down by a third, but he has done much more than that. He has changed its voice, or rather given it one. He has moved it from one rhetorical domain, The Official Style of economics and business, to another, less restrictive one, the middle style of ordinary written conversation, one which we can all share, which is to say, all understand. It may well be that writing like the revision would hurt your career chances as an economist, but isn't economics, as well as the rest of us, the poorer therefore?

You must, if you are to write prose in an America and a world fated to become ever more bureaucratic, learn how to use The Official Style, even perhaps how to enjoy it, without becoming imprisoned by it. You must manage to remember who is on first base, even if often you will not want to let on that you know. Long ago, La Rochefoucauld in his book of *Maxims* defined "a grave manner" as "a mysterious carriage of the body to cover defects of the mind." The Official Style has elevated this into an article of faith. Here is a sociological sample collected by Malcolm Cowley, with his translation:

In effect, it was hypothesized that certain physical data categories including housing types and densities, land use characteristics, and ecological location constitute a scalable content area. This could be called a continuum of residential desirability. Likewise, it was hypothesized that several social data categories, describing the same census tracts, and referring generally to the social stratification system of the city, would also be scalable. This scale would be called a continuum of socio-economic status. Thirdly, it was hypothesized that there would be a high positive correlation between the scale types on each continuum.

Here's the translation:

Rich people live in big houses set further apart than those of poor people. By looking at an aerial photograph of any American city, we can distinguish the richer from the poorer neighborhoods. (LF 65%)

("Sociological Habit Patterns in Linguistic Transmogrification," *The Reporter*, September 20, 1956.)

Such prose seems to aim at being scientific but actually wants to be priestly, to cast a witch doctor's spell. To translate the prose into a plain style—that is, to revise it into ordinary English—breaks the spell and defeats the purpose. Revision here becomes an act of satire.

THE RETURN OF POETIC DICTION

We face the euphemistic habit again here, but on a larger scale this time. The Official Style always wants to make things seem better than they are, more mysterious and yet somehow more controlled, more inevitable. It strives, at all times, both to disarm and to impress us. It suggests that it sees the world differently—sees, even, a different world. It suggests that those who see in this way form a charmed circle. Now such a use of language does not, to students of literature, sound unfamiliar. It is called *poetic diction*. And this is what The Official Style amounts to—a kind of poetic diction. *Here we come to the main problem with The Official Style.* There is no point in reproaching it for not being clear. It does not really want to be clear. It wants to be *poetic*. At its best, it wants to tell you *how it feels to be an official*, to project the sense of numinous self-importance officialdom confers. It wants to make a prosaic world mysterious.

I know, I know. It doesn't do it very well. But that's not the point. Until we see what it is trying to do, we can neither understand it nor translate it with any pleasure. Maybe a comparison from another time and context will make the point clearer. Here is a series of plain-language translations of Official Style poetic diction that the English poet Alexander Pope compiled for a satire on false poetic sublimity called *Peri Bathous* (1728). He gives first the poetic diction and then the ordinary language equivalent.

Poetic Diction	*Plain English*
For whom thus rudely pleads my loud-tongued gate, That he may enter? . . .	Who knocks at the Door?
Advance the fringed curtains of thy eyes, And tell me who comes yonder . . .	See who is there?
The wooden guardian of our privacy Quick on its axle turn . . .	Shut the Door.
Bring me what Nature, tailor to the *Bear*, To Man himself denied: She gave me Cold But would not give me Clothes . . .	Bring my Clothes.
Bring forth some remnant of *Promethean* theft, Quick to expand th'inclement air congealed By *Boreas'* rude breath . . .	Light the Fire.
Yon Luminary amputation needs, Thus shall you save its half-extinguished life.	Snuff the Candle.
Apply thine engine to the spongy door, Set *Bacchus* from his glassy prison free, And strip white *Ceres* of her nut-brown coat.	Uncork the Bottle, and chip the Bread.

And here is a modern version of such a list, culled from

an environmental impact statement filed by the FAA. I have
added the headings and the Plain English translation.

Poetic Diction	Plain English
limited in length	short
small faunal species	rats
experience growth	grow
annoyance factors	annoyances
police protection services	police
aircraft with lower noise emission characteristics	quieter planes
overlain by impervious surfaces	paved
exotic effluents	chemicals
weedy species	weeds
stepwise methodology	method
pollutant emissions control strategies	smog filters
olfactory impact	smell

Here is yet another glossary, an unintentional self-satire
this time, issued by the U.S. Office of Education (1971).
(Again, the headings are mine, but this time the Plain English
equivalents have been supplied by the Office of Education
itself, to prevent self-bewilderment.)

Poetic Diction	Plain English
Allocation of personnel and logistic resources to accomplish an identifiable objective. Activities constitute the basis for defining personnel assignments and for scheduling system operations.	Activity
The splitting of an entity into its constituent parts and the determination of relations among the parts and groups of the components.	Analysis

Production and refinement of a system or a product through trial-revision until it accomplishes its specified objectives.	Development
Those things (actions) that must be done to accomplish the overall job are referred to as functions.	Functions
To carry out. To fulfill. To give practical effect to and ensure of actual fulfillment by concrete measures.	Implement
Enhanced performance on any important dimension without detriment to the other essential dimensions.	Improvement
The job to be done, be it a product, a completed service, or a change in the condition of something or somebody.	Mission
A discrepancy or differential between "what is" and "what should be" (i.e., "what is required" or "what is desired"). In educational planning, "need" refers to problems rather than solutions, to the student "product" rather than to the resources for achieving that product, to the ends of education rather than to the means for attaining those ends.	Need
That toward which effort is directed. An intent statement and production for which a procedure is developed and resources allocated with a specific time frame and a measurable product signaling attainment.	Objectives
The organizational, procedural, technological, and support arrangements by which an agency has the capacity to	Planning Capability or Planning Competence

apply problem-solving processes to any problem that it may face.

Elements of a function that, when performed by people and things in proper sequential order, will or should resolve the parent function. Tasks may be performed by people, equipment, or people/ equipment combination.	Tasks

> (Robert A. Watson, "Making Things Perfectly Clear," *Saturday Review*, July 24, 1971.)

Imagine trying to *think* in a world speaking this language—a world where the simplest human activity is translated immediately into its most abstract equivalent and then immediately tossed into this gooey marmalade of pretentious tautology? This particular bureaucratic glossary was issued in the name of clarity, but doesn't it aim obviously at something else entirely? Doesn't it yearn for a playful, poetic, *ornamental* use of language? Those who use The Official Style seldom acknowledge the paradox, but you must feel its truth if you are not to make grotesque mistakes. Clarity is often the last thing The Official Style really wants to create and, if you find yourself in a bureaucratic context, often the last thing you want to create. A sociology paper or a corporate memo in plain English could spell disaster. You may well want, in marshaling your thoughts, to write out an ordinary language version. But you must then translate it into The Official Style. You must, that is, learn to read, write, and translate The Official Style as if it were a foreign language. Play games with it by all means, but don't get fooled by it.

Bureaucrats have, in the last few years, begun to do just this—play games with it. One government official, Philip Broughton, created something called the "Systematic Buzz Phrase Projector." It consists of three columns of words:

Column 1	*Column 2*	*Column 3*
0. integrated	0. management	0. options
1. total	1. organizational	1. flexibility
2. systematized	2. monitored	2. capability
3. parallel	3. reciprocal	3. mobility
4. functional	4. digital	4. programming
5. responsive	5. logistical	5. concept
6. optional	6. transitional	6. time-phase
7. synchronized	7. incremental	7. projection
8. compatible	8. third generation	8. hardware
9. balanced	9. policy	9. contingency

(*Newsweek*, May 6, 1968.)

You think of any three numbers, 747 say, and then read off the corresponding words, "synchronized digital projection." It is a device to generate verbal ornament, a machine for poetic diction. In fact, computer programs for making poetry in just this random way now exist. Try making up a version for whatever business dialect of The Official Style you need to write. You can pick numbers the way you do for a lottery. Not only will it lend new resonance and authority to your prose, it will act as a multiplier, increasing length and weight. It also acts as a mechanical muse, generates inspiration, or at least serviceable instant flapdoodle. Produce a phrase by the three-number procedure, invent a sentence for it, and then spend a paragraph or two reflecting on what it might mean. Invent a reality to which the phrase can refer.

A SOCIETY AFRAID OF BEING SUED

The deepest origins of The Official Style—and it flourished as far back as the Roman empire—lie in the language of the law. And, more especially, in the style of *statutes*, in legal language at its most official, when it wants to be most numinous, most impressive, most priestly. This historical dimension of The Official Style has come to haunt American society as it becomes more and more litigious. We are all afraid of being sued. We think that if we write *statutorially*, we'll somehow not get sued, or at least not convicted. Yet this attempt at boilerplate almost always backfires. As with The Official Style, when you attempt to outlaw the playfulness of language, to *be clear and nothing else*, the poetic diction sneaks back in through the back door. We'll confront this contemporary problem, *the statutory temptation* we might call it, by looking at a section from the California Penal Code (Section 384a) which warns us not to pick the flowers along the freeway.

The general strategy of statutory argument is *iterative*; it wants to include, iterate, every possible case. Everything is to be spelled out, made perfectly clear, pushed beyond the need for interpretation. How does it work out in practice? Prose like this, though of immeasurable antiquity and precedent, often creates unintended effects.

> Every person who within the State of California willfully or negligently cuts, destroys, mutilates, or removes any tree or shrub, or fern or herb or bulb or cactus or flower, or huckleberry or redwood greens, or portion of any tree or shrub, or fern or herb or bulb or cactus or flower, or huckleberry or redwood greens, growing upon state or county highway rights-of-way, or who removes leaf mold thereon; provided, however, that the provisions of this section shall not be construed to apply to any employee of the state or of any political subdivision thereof engaged in work upon any state, county or public road or highway while performing such work under the supervision of the state or of any political subdivision thereof, and every person who willfully or negligently cuts, destroys, mutilates or removes any tree or shrub, or fern or herb or bulb or cactus or flower, or huckleberry or redwood greens, growing upon public land or upon land not his own, or leaf mold on the surface of public land, or upon land not his own, without a written permit from the owner of the land signed by such owner or his authorized

agent, and every person who knowingly sells, offers, or exposes for sale, or transports for sale, any tree or shrub, or fern or herb or bulb or cactus or flower, or huckleberry or redwood greens, or portion of any tree or shrub, or fern or herb or bulb or cactus or flower, or huckleberry or redwood greens, or leaf mold, so cut or removed from state or county highway rights-of-way, or removed from public land or from land not owned by the person who cut or removed the same without the written permit from the owner of the land, signed by such owner or his authorized agent, shall be guilty of a misdemeanor and upon conviction thereof shall be punished by a fine of not more than five hundred dollars ($500) or by imprisonment in a county jail for not more than six months or by both such fine and imprisonment.

See what happens? The repetitions begin to sound like the formulas of epic poetry, pushing the whole passage toward the high style. And these repetitions make the passage sound like an Eastern religious chant, with its endless repetition of identical phrases. And at the same time, the mechanical appearance of the repetition makes the nonlawyer laugh, pushes the whole passage toward the low style. This passage represents The Official Style at its most formulaic. You can see how near it comes to turning into poetry. Let's reformat it as such, to dramatize its formulary mystery:

𝕰𝖛𝖊𝖗𝖞 𝖕𝖊𝖗𝖘𝖔𝖓 𝖜𝖍𝖔
within the State of California

willfully or negligently
   cuts,
      destroys,
         mutilates, or
            removes

[chorus]
   any tree or shrub, or fern or herb or bulb or cactus or

flower, or huckleberry or redwood greens,
　　　　　　or portion of
any tree or shrub, or fern or herb or bulb or cactus or
flower, or huckleberry or redwood greens,

growing upon state or county highway rights-of-way, or
　　who removes leaf mold thereon;

(provided, however, that

the provisions of this section shall not be construed to apply to
　　　　any employee **of the state**
　　or of any political subdivision thereof
　　　　engaged in work **upon any state**,
county or public road or highway while performing such work
　　under the supervision **of the state**
　　or of any political subdivision thereof),

and **every person who**
willfully or negligently
　　cuts,
　　　　destroys,
　　　　　　mutilates, or
　　　　　　removes

[chorus]

　　any tree or shrub, or fern or herb or bulb or cactus or
　　flower, or huckleberry or redwood greens,
　　　　　　　or portion of
　　any tree or shrub, or fern or herb or bulb or cactus or
　　flower, or huckleberry or redwood greens,

　growing upon public **land** or
　　　　　　upon **land** not his **own**,
　　　or leaf mold on the surface
　　　　　of public **land**, or

upon **land** not his own,
without a written permit from the **owner**
of the **land**
signed by such **owner**
or his authorized agent,

and **every person who**
knowingly
sells,
offers, or
exposes for sale, or
transports for sale,

[chorus]

any tree or shrub, or fern or herb or bulb or cactus or
flower, or huckleberry or redwood greens,
or portion of
any tree or shrub, or fern or herb or bulb or cactus or
flower, or huckleberry or redwood greens, or leaf mold,

so cut or **removed** from state or county highway rights-of-way,
or **removed** from public **land**
or from **land** not owned by the person
who cut or **removed** the same without the written permit from
the **owner** of the **land**,
signed by such **owner** or his authorized agent,

shall be guilty of a misdemeanor
and upon conviction thereof
shall be punished
by a fine of not more than five hundred dollars ($500) or
by imprisonment in a county jail for not more than six months
or **by** both such fine and imprisonment.

I have converted this excerpt from the California Penal Code
into a postmodern poem. You are invited to read vertically as

well as horizontally (e.g., **state, removed, owner, land**). You are invited to skip sections or, as with the **chorus,** to repeat sections set to your own music. You are invited, above all, to make a game out of self-important solemnity, just as the postmodern painter Marcel Duchamp did by painting a mustache on the Mona Lisa. In the process of thus desecrating the law, I have also made it much easier to understand. You can pick out the formulaic repetitions. You can see (gulp!) that the whole enchilada is a single sentence, and what the subject and verb ("Every person shall be punished!") really are.

THE OFFICIAL STYLE SUMMARIZED

Let's run over the basic elements of The Official Style again.

1. It is built on nouns, vague, general nouns. These nouns are often of Latin derivation, "shun" words like fixa*tion*, func*tion*, construc*tion*, educa*tion*, organiza*tion*, op*tion*, implementa*tion*, or other perennial favorites like flexibility, capability, concept, and so on.

2. These nouns are often, as in Broughton's game, modified by adjectives made up from other nouns like them, as in "incremental throughput" or "functional input."

3. All action is passive and impersonal. No active verbs and no direct objects. Never "I decided to fire him" but "It has been determined that the individual's continued presence in the present personnel configuration would tend to be to the detriment of the ongoing operational efficiency of the organizational unit in which the individual is currently employed."

4. Nothing is called by its ordinary name. You don't decide to bomb a town; instead, "It has been determined to maintain an aggressive and operational attack pos-

ture." You don't set up an office, you "initiate an on-going administrative facility."

5. The status quo is preserved in syntax. All motion is converted into stasis. The Official Style denies, as much as possible, the reality of action. You don't dis-like someone, you "maintain a posture of disapproval toward" him. You don't decide to hire someone, you "initiate the hiring process." You add all necessary qualifications by stringing together prepositional phrases rather than by careful word choice or use of the possessive case. Above all, you make the simple sound complex, as in the following prizewinner.

An Official Style Oscar

Official Style	*Plain English*
The purpose of this project is to develop the capability for institutions of higher learning and community agencies and organizations to coalesce for the development of community services that would maximize the available resources from a number of institutions and provide communication between priority needs and the responses of the educational needs of a given community.	This project aims to teach universities and community organizations how to work more efficiently together.

You can see the problem here. The plain English sounds *too simple*. A worthy project, no doubt, but who would ever fund anything as obvious as that?

We have, then, two weapons to combat The Official Style, not just one. We can *revise* it, as we have been doing in earlier chapters. Or, we can *play games with it*, as we have been doing here. We can banquet off the stuffiness of the prose itself. For, though it doesn't know it, and would deny it if charged,

The Official Style aspires not to clarity but to poetry—the poetry of bureaucracy—and we can analyze it as such, just as I have done here. Both PM translation and poetic analysis should help you translate into and out of The Official Style when needed.

Writing on an electronic screen, using typographical rearrangement and reemphasis, lets us deploy both weapons at once. We can puncture the pomposity while we clarify the meaning. It is to these revisionary powers of the electronic screen that we must now turn.

CHAPTER 5

ELECTRONIC LITERACY AND THE WORKPLACE

When you display written words on an electronic screen rather than imprint them on paper, reading itself changes radically; electronic "literacy" turns out to differ in fundamental ways from "print" literacy. And electronic literacy increasingly dominates the workplace. Anyone working in the business world confronts these radical changes in expressive medium, in "literacy," in reading and writing, every day. Even a practical hands-on guide like *Revising Business Prose* must pause to reflect on these changes, for they have transformed how the written word lives and works in business life.

EASY STREET

Changes close to home first. We have already noticed how word processors enhance prose revision. They make it much easier not only to get the words "down" ("on screen" not "on paper"!) but to take them up and move them around. And the speed with which revision takes place means, often, that more revision can take place when writing—as we usually do— under a deadline. No need to go through those one-day retyping turnarounds for each revision. And electronic spelling and grammar checkers and the electronic thesaurus, by speeding up ordinary procedures, further encourage revision. Global searches can find prepositional-phrase strings and tell you if every main verb is *is*. Use global search-and-replace to put a double space and carriage return at the end of each sentence for a page or two and you'll get a pretty good idea of sentence-length variation. Word-counters make computing the Lard Factor much faster. And changes in layout and typography become a handy analytical tool to find one's way in The Official Style's pathless prose woods. Because the computer is a rule-based device, it lends itself to a rule-based revision method. All in all, prose paramedics have never had it so easy.

WORDS AND IMAGES

But digital text has changed what we might call "business literacy" more profoundly than these helpful easements suggest. Most important, as anyone in business can now attest, the whole relationship between verbal and visual communication is changing. Images more and more both supplement and replace written information. Old-fashioned pie charts and bar graphs have given way to more imaginative and three-dimensional renderings of conceptual patterns. Even simple spreadsheet programs encourage the visualization of numeric data. And computer graphics now routinely model all kinds of complex dynamic processes in three dimensions and real time. We are so used to the convention of print—linear, regular left-to-right and top-to-bottom, black-and-white, constant font and type size—that we have forgotten how constraining it is. Black-and-white print is remarkable not only for its power to express conceptual thought but for all the powers it renounces in doing so. No pictures, no color, no perspective. Up to now these things have been just too expensive. No longer. On the electronic screen, you can do them all and a lot more. And as electronic memory gets ever cheaper, they have come within the reach not only of graphics designers but of everyday wordsmiths as well.

The constraints of conventionally printed prose are slowly dissolving. If we can use color, font size and shape, three-dimensional effects like drop-shadow and the like, then we will use them. If we can intersperse text and graphics with ease, we'll come to depend on the combination. All these changes, in their turn, are altering how we write and indeed how we think. It is no exaggeration to say that electronic textual information has now become three-dimensional. The black-and-white letters-only convention concentrates on abstract thought —the "meaning"—to the exclusion of everything else. Tonal colorations there will always be—they are what we usually call "style"—but in print they are always beneath the surface, implicit rather than explicit. Bringing them to the surface takes time and trouble, as we shall see in Chapter 6. With the electronic word, however, these tonal colorations can be explicit rather than implicit. We will be able, literally, to "color" our communications with one another. And there will be no going back, no abjuration of this new realm of communication. If you can write "in color," and choose not to, that too will be a "communication," and usually one you will not want to make. So don't be fooled by that black-and-white screen. How often nowadays do you watch black-and-white TV? And what does it seem like when you do?

VISUALIZATION AND SOUND

What do these changes imply for literacy in the workplace? Well, for a start, they dramatize a need I have been advocating all through this book, a need to use the visual imagination in reading, writing, and revising. More than ever, we must notice the shape of prose. Up to now, "graphics" people tended to work in one office and "word" people in another. No more. From now on, graphics will be fundamental to a writer's training. Words and images are now inextricably intertwined in our common expressive repertoire. The desktop-publishing revolution reinforces this change at every point. Typography and layout, a field heretofore restricted to editors and book designers, in electronic display become an expressive parameter for all writers. My students, to take one revealing example, now commonly choose a font for their papers to fit the course, teacher, or assignment. The classic creed of the typographer has always been that the written surface should be transparent—never noticed for itself, serving only the meaning shining through its lucid waters. That theory is in for some changes. We will be looking *at* the prose surface as much as looking *through* it.

I've also been arguing that prose—now uniformly read in silence—should be *voiced*, at least in the auditory imagination. The digitized word reinforces and empowers this recommendation as well. Since the last edition of this book, voice communication has become a reality in computer communication. We can now talk to the computer and it can talk back. It will not be long before voicing will be a routine dimension of the electronic word. We will move from voice to writing to image and back again in ways new to humankind. The Official Style pushes prose to its voiceless extreme. We have seen that over and over; *read it aloud* and The Official Style sounds silly, absurdly pompous, often simply pointless. Voice is now returning to writing in ways so fundamental as to recall an oral culture rather than a written one. *Voiceless* prose just won't work much longer.

Computer programs now exist to make this new mixture of word, image, and sound easier to pursue. The same digitized information, to begin with, can be expressed as either word, sound, or picture. I own a cheap but wonderful program (Laurie Spiegel's *Music Mouse*) which allows me to make music by drawing patterns on my mouse pad. Another one (*Jam Session*) allows me to play along with different music groups, according to definite but adjustable musical boundary conditions, by typing on my computer keyboard. Ordinary commercial programs like these form but the trickle-down residue of a fundamental information revolution; information from different parts of the human sensorium now shares a common digital code.

Plato dreamed of such a union, hoping to find the common center for all knowledge in mathematics. Ordinary marketplace training now embodies it. Interactive videodisc technology, a basic format for much business and military training, mixes sight and sound, word and image, as part of its standard operating procedure. Computer-assisted design and manufacturing programs regularly employ three-dimensional visual modeling as a fundamental conceptual tool. An entire new field of scientific creativity, called (appropriately enough) visualization, has been built about computer modeling techniques. And, on a more trivial desktop level, we are all inundated by CD-ROMs full of clip art.

Workplace electronic literacy, then, will differ markedly from workplace print literacy. It will mix alphabetic information with information coming from image and sound. Workers at every level will communicate in a richer but more complex informational sensorium. Writing will mean something different, and writers who don't know and feel this will find themselves the clerks of a forgotten mood.

AUTHORITY

Other changes fundamental to a business environment come with the electronic word. Perhaps foremost, *authority* changes. Although we seldom think of it thus, the print medium is fundamentally authoritarian. "In print" means authoritative. This penumbra of authority goes back a long way. The Renaissance humanists resurrected the authority of classical Greek and Latin culture by editing that culture's documents into fixed printed texts. The authoritative edition means the unchanging edition, text fixed forever, a lodestone of cultural authority. We still feel that way about print. It *fixes* things. Electronic text *unfixes* them. It is by nature changeable, anti-authoritarian. If we don't like what it says, we can change it, ornament it, revise it, erase it, mock it in letters indistinguishable from the original ones.

No one, so far as I know, has studied how print itself, as a technology, has influenced the history of managerial authority, but it must have done so. And that technology-based managerial authority is now changing. Ask any teacher of a computer-lab course or network administrator. She'll tell you about the big change—the teacher is no longer the *teacher*, the supervisor no longer in charge. The patterns of authority have shifted, become democratized. This democratization means that the electronic word will mean something very different in business from the printed one. Anyone interested in business writing must understand this change.

It operates, for a start, upon the very role the writer adopts as a writer. When we write we inevitably adopt a social role of some sort. Trying to bring this presentation of self to self-consciousness has been one of our main tasks in this book. Surely all of us have noticed that the kind of self we adopt in computer communication, especially on-line and, to a lesser degree, in electronic mail, differs from our "print" self. I'm not altogether sure why, but it does seem true. For reasons I will leave to the psychologists, computers have from their beginnings evoked the game and play ranges of human motivation far more strongly than print. The whole hacker personality that created the computer was suffused with the competitive game impulse, but equally with the "for-its-own-sake" impulse just to do something to see if it could be done. Some of this hacker mentality seems inevitably to creep in whenever we put our fingers on the computer's home row: we hold language more lightly in our hands; our sense of humor stands closer. A good predisposition this turns out to be—returning from theory to home concerns—for avoiding The Official Style and its systematic pomposity. The "dignity of print" has a lot to answer for. Let's hope that the electronic word preserves the muse of comedy that has hovered around its creation. At all events, it is something to be alert to if you are writing and revising business prose in an electronic office. It has created a new kind of communications decorum.

VOLATILE TEXT; VOLATILE MARKETS

I've talked a little earlier about the "allegory" of typographical change. By this, I've meant that font choice can be as revealing as word choice, that typographical layout can express your meaning as clearly as sentence layout. How a printed verbal surface *looks*, that is, affects how it *means*. We can allegorize the instability and volatility of electronic display in the same kind of way. If we ask what attributes the business world now agrees businesspeople should have, the list might go something like this:

- Knowledge of the field, but not encylopedic knowledge so much as an ability to locate and apply needed knowledge quickly.
- Adaptability to rapidly changing circumstances.
- Macrocosmic perspective; ability to take the global view.
- Microcosmic perspective; ability to control costs in fine detail.
- Ability to move from macrocosm to microcosm and back quickly; an ability, that is, *to change scale* in how we think.
- Ability to recognize *fixed attitudes* for what they are, in oneself and others, and to change them.
- Sensitivity to world markets; that is to say, sensitivity to other cultures, other social styles, to the "concept and feel" of different national and cultural patterns of consumption.
- An ability to manage without the authoritarian panoply that has so often accompanied management in the past.

(When I was in the military, this used to be called the "leading" rather than the "pushing" theory of command.)

Can we not say that, in some ways, fixed print works against all these abilities? It fixes the reader into a single scale—writers of fixed text can hardly do anything else. It tries to nail down reality—that's what getting it into print means. And might we not say that the intrinsic volatility of electronic text (using *text* now to mean the whole mixed range of word/sight/sound signals we have just discussed) enhances these abilities? The stylistic clues of different computer-user interfaces—that "total concept and feel" which has become a legal criterion now being applied in computer copyright cases—model how cultures differ. The ability to *change scale*, to zoom in and out, provides one of the primary computer enhancements to human sensory apparatus. The volatility of electronic text, its fundamental changeability, models for us a marketplace which is always changing, never fixed in print. The rules of today will not be the rules of tomorrow. And that changeability means that authority, though always necessary, must be held with a more delicate hand, and democratized as much as circumstance allows.

I don't want to extend further this argument about the deep expressive symbolism of computer display because *Revising Business Prose* is not a theoretical book, either about prose or management. But as much as I have said must, I think, be said now whenever business writing is discussed. The electronic word has changed the whole matrix of written expression, just as digitization has transformed the marketplace itself. To ignore this state change at the one level is as perilous as to ignore it at the other.

THE FUTURE OF "BUSINESS ENGLISH"

Business news is full of predictions these days about the changes that an "information society" will bring. Let me end these brief but needful reflections with one that emerges from our labors at prose revision. The logic of a society built on information instead of, or in addition to, goods, will lead us to a self-consciousness about words and the signals they broadcast far greater than now customary in the business world. The kind of verbal self-consciousness that now seems restricted to writers and literary critics will, by the very technological "logic" of an electronic information society, become a central management skill. In the past, "business English" has sometimes been taken to mean a special dialect of English restricted to the verbal formulas of trade, rather than what it really is, a language that ranges as widely as the spirit of commerce. Business in an information society will no longer be able to write "Business English"—if it ever did. It will need "English" of every sort—and lots of other languages besides. "Business English" may turn out to be the most protean kind of English on the worldwide stage. This new conception of business prose—as wide as language itself, and as bright and sparkling and changeable as the electronic word can make it—offers a new and lively path whose ending none of us can foresee.

CHAPTER 6

THE PERILS OF REVISION

Macpherson v. Texas Department of Water Resources

It is much easier to revise prose in a classroom or a textbook than on the job; no context qualifies your red pencil or your cursor. When you are actually doing business, things are rarely so simple. The memo you are revising was written by your boss, or by a touchy but valuable subordinate. Or a customer. Or a competitor. The social and political situation governs what you can and what you want to do. The bigger the organization, the more complex the social situation in which writing occurs. Big corporations and government bureaus often have style sheets, publicly proclaimed definitions of "good prose," as well as many tacit but strong conventions. You must obey them. Often you want simply to remain anonymous. When I was drafted into the army a friend who had been there counseled me to find the biggest group I could and jump right into the middle of it. Good advice, and not

only for the army. Often an itch for survival will blend you
right into the woodwork. If people in that woodwork write
The Official Style, you had better facilitate your prose utilization in the same way. If you want to get a contract from the
Bureau of Naval Ordnance, you'll write the kind of language
they understand there.

But, as we have seen, there are good reasons to avoid The
Official Style when you can. You'll save your company some
time and money more likely than not, and often a good deal
of trouble as well. You must remember, though, that writing
is a very "love me, love my dog" personal kind of thing. It
represents the public self of the writer and you must treat
it accordingly. In the short drama of revision that we explore
in this chapter—"Macpherson v. Texas Department of Water
Resources"—Ms. Macpherson forgot this cardinal rule and lost
her job for it. The incident took place in a government agency
rather than in business, but the lessons of writing and management that it teaches apply so directly to business writing that
we are going to conclude our prose revision labors by studying
it in detail. It richly repays such study. Here is the case as
reported by the Appellate Court. It provides a brilliant object
lesson in the relationships between prose style and political
power; it delineates, that is to say, business writing in its natural habitat.

MACPHERSON v. DEPT OF WATER RESOURCES
U.S. Court of Appeals,
Fifth Circuit (New Orleans)

*MACPHERSON v. TEXAS DEPARTMENT OF WATER
RESOURCES, et al., No. 83–1692, June 25, 1984*

CIVIL RIGHTS ACT OF 1964
   Sex   Discharge   108.4112
      105.5101
         Finding that state agency discharged female employee because
      of her pertness in appending to memorandum specific and gen-
      eral comments designed to inform its author of his literary

ineptitude and in then sending memorandum back to executive director, who originally sent memorandum over his signature, and not because of her gender is not clearly erroneous, where evidence supports conclusion that final decision to discharge the reviser was made before director discovered that female employee, who had received more promotions and merit raises than any other employee in her section, was the reviser.

Appeal from the U.S. District Court for the Western District of Texas. Affirmed.

Leonard J. Schwartz and Katherine L. Moore (Waterman & Schwartz), Austin, Tex., for appellant.

Jim Mattox, Attorney General of Texas, and Evelyn S. Tatum, Assistant Attorney General, for appellee.

Before GEE, POLITZ, and JOHNSON, Circuit Judges.

Full Text of Opinion

GEE, Circuit Judge:—This appeal concerns whether Ms. Gwendolyn Macpherson was dismissed from her position with an agency of the State of Texas for a wrong reason: being female. In a bench trial, the court gave judgment for the defendant, entering detailed findings of fact and conclusions of law. On the peculiar facts of the case, we conclude that one of his findings— which is supported by the record evidence—is dispositive, so that we need not look beyond it to affirm.

The record indicates that Ms. Macpherson is a graduate geologist of high intelligence, independent mind and—one may infer—somewhat venturesome spirit. Employed by a predecessor department of the defendant agency in March 1976, she established an enviable work record, marred by only a single verbal reprimand for climbing a fence to examine certain deposits on private property without obtaining the landowner's permission. During her brief tenure with the state, she received more promotions and merit raises than any other employee in her section.

In September 1977, her department was merged with two other state water agencies to become the present defendant agency and defendant Harvey Davis became executive director of the new entity. One may infer from the record that in the months immediately following the merger Davis was strained by the inevitable tensions consequent to his new position and the effort to harmonize his amalgamated charges into a functional entity.

In January 1978, Mr. Davis circulated a memorandum over his signature to his division directors within the agency. The memo had actually been prepared by a staff attorney and was entitled "Outside Requests of [*sic*] Staff Testimony at Administrative and Judicial Hearings." Like the title, portions of it were poorly worded. Ms. Macpherson determined that it required grammatical and stylistic improvement. She therefore proceeded to correct Mr. Davis's memo in searching detail, appending both specific and general comments calculated to bring home to the author his literary ineptitude. Her final observation fairly gives the flavor of the whole:

> You frequently leave out articles (a, an, the) in front of nouns. You tend to obfuscate by using long, unwieldy phraseology. Simplify! Simplify! This will help correct your tendency to misplace modifiers. The content of this memo is confusing. It is obvious to me that when one is subpoenaed one must appear, regardless of the opinion of the Department. Furthermore, one must tell the truth when under oath.
>
> Please rewrite and resubmit.[1]

She then anonymously mailed her revision to Mr. Davis in an envelope marked "personal," and thus it came directly to his hand.

While adhering to the ceiling of his office, revised memo in hand, Mr. Davis determined to fire the reviser, whomever [*sic*] he or she might be. As the trial court chastely put it in Finding of Fact No. 16, "The termination decision was made prior to the discovery of the identity of the employee who revised the memo and anonymously sent it to Mr. Harvey Davis." After an investigation in the course of which she readily admitted the

---

[1] The memo and Mrs. Macpherson's corrections and comments are reproduced in full at the foot of our opinion.

revision and anonymous return of the memo,[2] and a meeting between Mr. Davis and the director of Ms. Macpherson's division, her immediate supervisor, and the agency general counsel, Davis reiterated his decision that the reviser, her identity now known, should be dismissed and she was.

As we note above, the trial court, to whose opportunity to hear and view the witnesses we must defer, concluded that a final decision to discharge the reviser was made before her identity became known. The record contains evidence that supports this finding, as well as evidence to support a determination that the initial decision was tentative and became final only after she was discovered. It is not for us, however, to second-guess the trial court's credibility choices among differing pieces of testimony—even those coming from the same witness or witnesses—unless a review of the record leaves us "with the definite and firm conviction that a mistake has been committed." United States v. United States Gypsum Co., 333 U.S. 364, 395, 68 S. Ct. 525, 92 L.Ed. 746 (1948), reh'g denied, 333 U.S. 869, 68 S.Ct. 788, 92 L.Ed. 1147. That is not the case today, and the finding must stand.

Since the decision to fire Ms. Macpherson was taken when her identity, and perforce her gender, were unknown and merely carried out after they were discovered, there can be no question of sex discrimination on this record. There it ends.

In closing, we observe that although the unique facts of today's case lend themselves irresistibly to somewhat ironic treatment, we do not view lightly the small bureaucratic tragedy that the record reveals: a harried executive has lost his temper and a valuable—if somewhat pert—state employee has lost her position. On this record, however, we cannot hold the trial judge clearly erroneous in finding that it was Ms. Macpherson's pertness and not her gender that cost her the job she held. We do not sit to revise employment decisions taken hastily or for insuf-

---

[2] Adding, according to the testimony of her immediate supervisor, that "she just could not stand the idea that an Executive Director of an agency like that putting out a memo that was in such bad form grammatically and that something to the effect that she really didn't like to work for anybody like that." (Tr. 135).

ficient reasons, only those taken for illegal ones. And so, with all sympathy and good wishes for the future of Ms. Macpherson, we conclude that the trial court's judgment must be AFFIRMED.[3]

Let's begin by looking at the original memo, as annotated by Ms. Macpherson, which caused all the trouble. It begins, as do all memos, with a schematic heading:

TO: All Division Directors
THRU:
FROM: Harvey Davis, Executive Director
SUBJECT: Outside Requests of Staff Testimony at Administrative and Judicial Hearings

All very boring formulaic stuff, it seems. But what is really going in this—or any—memo heading? What do you learn from it as a reader? What constraints does it impose upon you as a writer? First, the routing instructions define your audience for you, and much more explicitly than writers can usually know. Here is your readership. Of course others may come to read it (it is directed to Division Directors and Ms. Macpherson was not, so far as we know, a Division Director), but the target audience is fully known. For you the writer, this will preempt many decisions—tone, stylistic level, length, and so on. And as the reader, you will know how to read the memo; its genre, or literary type, will have been defined for you. You'll know with what kind of salt to take it. Harvey Davis was a senior boss, a boss of bosses, an Executive Director. That tells you a lot. He was also new on the job, and that tells you a lot more. He may not know his audience, after all, very well, even though he knows who they are. That will have to wait upon experience in the job. But he clearly writes from a position of power; that position will form part of any response to the memo. No reader can pretend not to know *who wrote it.*

---

[3] In anticipation of a critical review of our remarks, we have been at some pains with their style and grammar.

The SUBJECT heading conveys two very different kinds of messages. On the surface, it tells us the subject of the memo: "Outside Requests of Staff Testimony at Administrative and Judicial Hearings." Beneath the surface, it casts grave doubt on the writer's linguistic competence. The writer means "Outside Requests *for* Staff Testimony." Someone is requesting the staff members to testify. But he doesn't say that. Instead, he makes a mistake in English idiom, using a unidiomatic preposition, "of," to mean "for." A trifling mistake, though, like mistaking "disinterested" for "uninterested"? Not at all. To make a mistake in idiom means you don't dwell in the family of native English speakers. It is a very small but very revealing error. It puts you outside a very large but very important group. Like a mistake in manners, it affects the observer out of all proportion to its intrinsic importance. (It does make a difference, of course, since it means something different from what the writer intends it to mean, but enough redundancy is built into the message so we can see around the mistake.) The writer has lost his authority before he has begun. He has put himself in the penalty box, labeled "to be corrected." Ms. Macpherson did not, as it happens, correct this error, but she is alert to errors of idiomatic preposition, for she corrects one later on; an incorrect "of" is changed to an idiomatic "about." The mistake in the heading establishes her role vis-à-vis the writer, a role strongly at odds with the boss-subordinate one. Smart subordinates don't fall into this trap, but smart bosses don't set it, either.

Now, before we look at the memo in detail, stand back from it and look at it *cum commento*, with all its marginal annotations. What does it remind you of? Yep. That's right. One of those papers you wrote in freshman English. Ms. Macpherson removes the memo from its original dramatic context and puts it in another play, one in which she is the teacher and good old Harv Davis finds himself sitting in the corner wearing a dunce cap. It is this reversal that makes him hit the ceiling and fire her on the spot, not what she says about his prose. He does not sit down and ponder his mistakes in unidiomatic

Texas Department of Water Resources

INTEROFFICE MEMORANDUM

TO   : All Division Directors   DATE: January 16, 1978
THRU :
FROM : Harvey Davis, Executive Director
SUBJECT: Outside Requests of Staff Testimony at Administrative and
          Judicial Hearings

[handwritten: stipulates that:]

Section 5.173 of the Texas Water Code ~~provides:~~

> "[the] position of and information developed by the department shall
> be presented by the executive director or his designated representative
> at hearings of the board and the commission and at hearings held by
> federal, state, and local agencies on matters affecting the public's
> interest in the state's water resources, including matters that have
> been determined to be policies of the state. The executive director
> shall be named a party in hearings before the commission."

[handwritten annotation: Always write out abbreviation before]

The position of the Executive Director is developed during application review by
legal and technical staff and formalized prior to submission of the application
and the recommendation of the Executive Director to the Commission for setting
of a contested (APA) hearing. Obviously, disagreements will arise among a
professional staff of the position that should be taken. However, absent the
development of previously unknown information during the hearing process
which materially affects the recommendation, each representative is expected
to advocate the position taken. Occasionally, other parties to a hearing will seek the testimony of Department
employees, either because of general expertise or because of knowledge relating
to an application developed in the review process. Any employee of the Department who is requested or subpoenaed to appear to present testimony at any public
hearing, administrative or judicial, relative to his official duties with the
agency must immediately notify the Executive Director of such request upon receipt.
We will then be able to review the request with ample time to determine a course
of action. All employees who testify in public hearings, whether called on
behalf of the Executive Director or by another party, are expected to fully
and truthfully answer all questions.

[handwritten annotations:]
- subject / verb
- This does not make sense. One sets a hearing date.
- This implies that a hearing is set only when application is contested.
- This makes staff singular—cannot use "among"
- ABOUT
- BY WHOM? Needs object.
- WHOSE? needs possessive adjective like "their"
- misplaced modifier—place it next to "information"
- misplaced modifier—place it next to "development"
- POOR WORDING CHOICE! Perhaps you mean "bearing"
- Is the Executive Director more than one person? Webster says: "we, used as I by sovereigns, by writers to keep an impersonal character." "we" is not appropriate here.
- AWKWARD These should be reversed.
- Comment concerning content: The course of action is determined in next sentence, and needs no review by the Executive Director.
- Misplaced modifier— Application was not developed in the review process, but knowledge was.
- nonparallel construction. AWKWARD as well.

THE PERILS OF REVISION

-2-   January 16, 1978

Comment concerning contact. Is the Dept. impartial? Ever? I thought only the commission was impartial.

Who refuses this acceptance of fees and expenses?

In general, upon request from an outside person, the Department will provide the
expert witness on state time and at state expense to impartially provide
information to the judge or examiner, rather than to allow a litigant to call
a Department employee as his witness. The refusal of employee's acceptance
of witness fees and travel expenses, even where provided by law, will help
insure impartiality. However, a case by case determination of utilization of
State travel monies will be made by this Office to insure the reasonableness
of the request in light of the requested employee's expertise and the relation
of the subject of the lawsuit to the statutory responsibilities of the
Department.

Is the refusal provided by law? The acceptance? Or the fees and expenses?

Harvey Davis

What request?

This is the first time a lawsuit has been mentioned. I thought this memo concerned public hearings.

Overall comments
    You frequently leave out articles
(a, an, the) in front of nouns. You tend to
obfuscate by using long, unwieldly,
phraseology. Simplify! Simplify!
This will help correct your tendency
to misplace modifiers. The content of
this memo is confusing. It is obvious
to me that when one is subpoenaed
one must appear, regardless of the
opinion of the Department. Furthermore,
one must tell the truth when under oath.
Please rewrite and resubmit

prepositions, lament, or vaunt, misplacing his modifier. He responds not to a prose revision but to the power reversal that it implies. This reversal is implied, to one degree or another, by every act of revision and no reviser should ever forget it. We schoolteachers often do, for after all, we are the ones in power and so don't feel threatened. Revising prose is first, and often foremost, an act of political power. Forget this and you may, like Ms. Macpherson, find yourself out of a job.

Her comments, questions, and corrections are, with a couple of exceptions, sensible and helpful. They are also, with no exceptions, insufferably schoolteacherish and superior in tone. The concluding comment—that great occasion for displays of professorial humor—takes the cake:

> You frequently leave out articles (a, an, the) in front of nouns. [Again, the revealing error in English idiom.] You tend to obfuscate by using long, unwieldy phraseology. Simplify! Simplify! This will help correct your tendency to misplace modifiers. The content of this memo is confusing. It is obvious to me [note the stress on "to me"] that when one is subpoenaed one must appear, regardless of the opinion of the Department. Furthermore, one must tell the truth when under oath. Please rewrite and resubmit.

Zowie! The tonal coloration accompanying this bracing criticism goes something like, "Boss, you really are a longwinded, semiliterate, lazy jerk. Try it again and try, if you can, to get it right this time." Ms. Macpherson was an exemplary employee in every other way. Could she have been this naive? Well, maybe not. Maybe she expected Davis to read her correction ironically, as a kind of laughing invocation of the teacher-pupil relationship to call attention to some (as we shall see later) very serious mistakes. Or maybe she just expected him to be sensible enough, and self-controlled enough, to accept the criticism for what it was worth (a lot, as it turns out) and ignore the tone. Or at least to find out who wrote it, and thus perhaps why, before acting. Ms. Macpherson's supervisor testified that Ms. Macpherson "just could not stand the idea that an Executive Director of an agency like that putting out a memo that was in such bad form grammatically and . . . that she did not really like to work for anybody like that." If so, she got her wish. But perhaps she thought that any sensible manager would call a subordinate in and set the power relation straight in private. After all, Ms. Macpherson had sent the message marked "personal" (the judge misses the point of this in his comment upon it) so that no one else would see it, and Mr. Davis would not be publicly humiliated.

The record does not conclusively support any of these possible interpretations. But we have to guess because motive so colors how the comments were made and so, finally, what those comments were, what "message" they were meant to convey. We always do this when we read. And we should always do it when we write. The meta-signals are often more significant than the surface ones.

And what do we learn about Harvey Davis from his response? Especially about Harvey Davis *as a manager*? A lot, and all of it bad. The bottom line is that he loses an excellent employee. Excellent employees are hard to find these days; excellent geologists willing to work for government wages, I would bet, even harder. After you cool down, you *read the revisions* that Anonymous contributed. You then find out who Anon. is and call him or her in for a confidential chat. Maybe you'll learn something else valuable about how your prose is being received in the office. Even tactless Anon. may be able to teach you some lessons in tone. And that's that. No lawsuit, no job to fill, no big fuss. Instead, Harvey's egotism forces him to publicize his humiliation. Parade his bad prose style.

And the prose style wasn't even his! "In January 1978, Mr. Davis circulated a memorandum over his signature to his division directors within the agency. The memo had actually been prepared by a staff attorney." Harvey feels not the wrath of a prose style scorned but *lese majesty*. The reviser has attacked not his prose but his position, his self-esteem. Like a medieval baron, he rages because someone has dared to strike his servant. The memo itself becomes simply a pawn in a power confrontation. The Court infers that Davis was "strained by the inevitable tensions consequent to his new position." Maybe so, but the real reason seems to be native insecurity and an ego the size of an elephant.

The writer's block, or writer's loathing maybe we should call it, which many businesspeople feel, often comes not from lack of something to say, or even hesitation about how to say it, but from fear. Fear that their memo will encounter a Harvey Davis somewhere up the line. The persistent euphemism that pervades business writing—have you ever noticed all the circumlocutions for "money" in corporate discourse?—comes from a fear of giving offense. As often as not, The Official Style is pressed into service not to fool people or parade pomposity but as an act of *piety*. People want to do the right thing. They want, at whatever cost to prose style or efficient communication, to behave properly.

The Paramedic Method offers no help here. Only wide and attentive reading will let you command the whole tonal range of prose and only tact and a keen social sense will create a prose that gets the message across in a way that soothes your boss rather than rattling her cage. People never write in a vacuum. This little lesson in management—for it is bad management as much as bad prose that stands at issue here—shows that business writing always has to work in a power structure and always function, in one way or another, as an element of that structure. When the boss tells you to be clear, be careful. She may not want you to be *that* clear.

Now, what about the prose that set off this land mine? It is legal prose, a memo drafted by a lawyer, citing a legal document (the *Texas Water Code*), giving instructions about testimony in court. This kind of litigious environment pervades business and government today, as we all know. As a result, the language of the law becomes a major force in business writing, a twin pincer that, with The Official Style, threatens to squeeze plain English out of even the simplest document. Legal language is a study in itself, and we haven't time for it here. (The classic work on the subject, for those who are interested, is David Mellinkoff's brilliant *The Language of the Law*, Boston: Little, Brown, 1963.) But the pressure to *sound* legalistic even if you are not a lawyer or drafting a statute has become relentless in business today. Everyone is afraid of being sued and legal-sounding language seems the only flak vest around.

Legal language at its worst has a lot in common with The Official Style. Look at the first sentence of the memo:

The position
   of the Executive Director
is developed
during application review
by legal and technical staff and formalized
prior to submission
of the application and the recommendation
of the Executive Director
to the Commission
for setting
of a contested APA hearing.

Our standard Official Style formula. No focus. No rhythm. No emphasis. No voice. Hard to read. It is riddled with mistakes, as Ms. Macpherson points out, but misplaced modifiers and unidiomatic prepositions are not the main problems. It is the vices of The Official Style, the endless, shapeless, actionless shopping-bag sentences, that drag it down. Try a PM number on it. What comes out, finally, is some dangerous advice. Employees will tell the truth when under oath, of course, but once the position of the Executive Director has been decided upon "each representative is expected to advocate the position taken." This comes perilously close to counseling perjury, as Ms. Macpherson tries to point out in her closing comment: "It is obvious to me that when one is subpoenaed one must appear, regardless of the opinion of the Department. Furthermore, one must tell the truth when under oath." This kind of shrewd observation a good boss ignores at his peril, however impertinently it may be wrapped up. For it points out the central contradiction of the memo, one that could get Harvey Davis in serious legal trouble.

Legal language usually defends itself by arguing that it must sacrifice elegance on the altar of clarity. But here the style becomes so official that sense is completely obscured. The strategy of legal language as self-defense has boomeranged, left the agency open to a legal peril it has created itself. If Ms. Macpherson had been able to wrap this point up in enough deference, perhaps Mr. Davis would have been able to see it and pass the criticism along to its real target, the staff attorney who wrote the memo in the first place.

Legal language need not confound itself in its own Official Style, of course. Just look at the splendid prose of Judge Gee's opinion. He does admit that he has paid attention to his prose: "In anticipation of a critical review of our remarks, we have been at some pains with their style and grammar." But the authority of his prose comes from tone, not good grammar. He must first show us that he, too, can see what is wrong with the memo, but notice how easily and indirectly he does so. Ms. Macpherson had neglected to remark the unidiomatic preposition in the memo's title but the judge does not; he simply puts a "[*sic*]" after it to mark the error without writing, as I did earlier, a song about it. He then comments on the memo: "Like the title, portions of it were poorly worded." He then makes plain the subtext of Ms. Macpherson's comments: "She . . . proceeded to correct Mr. Davis's memo in searching detail, appending both specific and general comments calculated to bring home to the author his literary ineptitude." He thus shows us that he can read both kinds of "content," establishing his credentials as a literary critic. At the same time, he is establishing his human judgment as well, his qualifications for his own job. From his tone flows his authority.

If Ms. Macpherson's prose revision stands disastrously at odds with its social context, the judge's sense of style fits its context exactly. Look at the contrast between how Judge Gee describes what happened and the trial court's Official Style version:

While adhering to the ceiling of his office, revised memo in hand, Mr. Davis determined to fire the reviser, whomever [*sic*] he or she might be.

The plain style, with an ironical allusion to The Official Style—"while adhering to the ceiling of his office"—that one might expect. Then the ever so slightly ironical introduction to the trial court's lumpen description:

> As the trial court chastely put it in Finding of Fact No. 16, "The termination decision was made prior to the discovery of the identity of the employee who revised the memo and anonymously sent it to Mr. Harvey Davis."

Judge Gee's language proves that he can both see a prose style and see through and around it. And the stylistic command is read as a judgmental command: he can read human behavior with equal skill and tact. He also knows, rarest of all, how to write a short sentence. And even, look at this, how powerful a short sentence will become when it follows a long one:

> Since the decision to fire Ms. Macpherson was taken when her identity, and perforce her gender, were unknown and merely carried out after they were discovered, there can be no question of sex discrimination on this record. There it ends.

I've spent so much time on this sad and funny case because it points so directly and economically to the context in which prose revision always occurs, the boundary conditions within which the PM must be applied. Applying it may be laborious but it is not arcane. Anyone can do it. This kind of revision can be formulaic because the prose it seeks to revise is formulaic, too. But there is nothing formulaic about when and how, and why, we do it. To answer those questions we must leave the schoolroom and depend on such native wit and good sense as any of us is lucky enough to possess.

CHAPTER 7

WHY BOTHER?

I've been arguing that much of our writing problem comes from the goals and attributes that make up The Official Style. We have seen what The Official Style looks like: dominantly a noun style; a concept style; a style whose sentences have no design, no shape, rhythm, or emphasis; an unreadable, voiceless, impersonal style; a style built on euphemism and various kinds of poetic diction; above all, a style with a formulaic structure, "is" plus a string of prepositional phrases before and after. But just because it is a formulaic style, we can use a formula to revise it into plain English. The Paramedic Method handles the problem nicely. We might usefully review it here:

1. Circle the prepositions.
2. Circle the "is" forms.
3. Ask, "Where's the action?" "Who's kicking who?"
4. Put this "kicking" action in a simple (not compound) active verb.
5. Start fast—no slow windups.
6. Write out each sentence on a blank sheet of paper and mark off its basic rhythmic units with a " / ".
7. Read the passage aloud with emphasis and feeling.
8. Mark off sentence lengths in the passage with a " / ".

To repeat: this formula does work, but it works only because the style it aims to revise is so formulaic to begin with. It really is a paramedic method, an emergency procedure. Don't confuse it with the art of medicine, with knowing about the full range of English prose styles—how to recognize and how to write them. That kind of knowledge is what English composition is all about. We are talking here about a subdivision of that broader field, about only one kind of stylistic revision. Because it is only one kind, it leaves a lot out.

Most obviously—as we've just seen with Ms. Macpherson—it leaves out time, place, and circumstance. It aims to be clear and brief, but often, if the social surface is to be preserved, clarity and brevity must be measured out in small doses. We seldom communicate only neutral information; we are incorrigibly interested in the emotions and human relationships that go with it.

WHY BOTHER? TWO KINDS OF ANSWERS

Because the Paramedic Method ignores this aspect of writing, it can get you into trouble. Well, then, you might well ask, "Why bother?" The kind of revision we've been doing is hard work. Why do it if it's only going to get us in trouble? Why sit in your office and feel foolish trying to read a memo aloud for rhythm and shape? If The Official Style is the accepted language of our bureaucratic world, why translate it into English? Why stand up when everyone else is sitting down? Questions to be asked, though to answer we'll have to go a step or two beyond paramedicine. There are two answers, really, or rather two kinds of answers—"efficiency" answers and "ego" answers.

Efficiency Answers

"Efficiency" first. A reader of an earlier version of this book made the main point for me:

"Why bother?" You omitted one of the most important reasons: cost.

Two years ago our new organization needed a Constitution and By-Laws, and a By-Laws Committee was appointed for the task. They found a sample from a similar organization, made title and other changes and produced the 12-page Constitution and By-Laws. That was not sufficient, however, and they were instructed to add more "management organization" to the Constitution. But then, of course, the By-Laws didn't agree with the expanded Constitution. One By-Laws amendment corrected one disparity, but others remained. It appeared to me that when the By-Laws were expanded to match the expanded Constitution, 19 pages of that format would be required. It was getting out of hand, and the reproduction costs could break our meager treasury.

A few months ago a friend told me about *Revising Prose*, and suggested its principles might be applied to By-Laws as much as to straight prose. I was skeptical at first but I zeroed-in on Who's Kicking Who, eliminating useless words, nonsense phrases, and needless repetition. And because we had never appointed all that added management organization, I simply eliminated them. The fever was catching, and I challenged myself to get it on four pages. To do that I used the left margin for headings and maximized print density by eliminating as much white area as possible. Our "lard factor" was perhaps as high as you've ever seen.

The result is our new-look Constitution and By-Laws with easily located subjects, quicker to read with improved comprehension, and technically more accurate.

One copy now costs 20 cents versus 60 cents in the original and 95 cents if we had culminated the expansions. At our most recent meeting on April 19, 1980, it was adopted unanimously with only one change: the part about Assessments was stricken completely because it had never been noticed before and, now that it was easy to see, the idea was unacceptable to the group!

A small instance for a large lesson. The cost—in money, time, and perplexity—exacted by The Official Style is literally and metaphorically incalculable. If we could calculate it, though, it would certainly be the difference between 20 cents and 60 cents, and maybe between 20 cents and 95 cents. A two-thirds savings of time and money! A four-fifths saving! Whew! Imagine this kind of saving in a large corporation or government agency. These numbers may seem extravagant, but the Lard Factor amounts to a deadly multiplier: my letter to you, two times as long as it needs to be, evokes a letter from you two times as long as mine and four times as long as the subject demands, and so on *ad infinitum*. In the context of this unforgiving multiplier, criteria like sentence shape, rhythm, and sound turn out to be less literary graces than cost-effective necessities. Reading aloud for rhythm may end up saving you money.

The reader's letter makes a second point as essential as the first—the back pressure that revision exerts on thought and imagination. Revising what we write constitutes a self-satire, a debate with ourselves. The Paramedic Method brings ideas out into the open, denies them the fulsome coloration of a special language. If the ideas are unacceptable, like the "Assessments" section of the By-Laws, we'll see this clearly. The Official Style encourages us to fool ourselves as well as other people, to believe in our own bureaucratic mysteries. The Paramedic Method puts our ideas back under real pressure. They can then develop and grow or—painful as this always is—find their way to the circular file. If translation into plain English reveals only banalities, it's back to the drafting board for fresh ideas. The great thing about the Paramedic Method is that it allows us to conduct this self-education in private.

We can, too, think of efficiency and writing in a slightly different, but not in the end less cost-effective, way. We live in an age of bureaucracy, of large and impersonal organizations, public and private. We're not likely to change this much. Size and impersonality seem unavoidable concomitants of the kind of global planning we'll increasingly have to do. But surely the task of language is to leaven rather than to echo this impersonality. It is a matter of efficiency as well as of humanity and aesthetic grace. We understand ideas better when they come, manifestly, from other human beings. That is simply the way human understanding evolved. It is people, finally, who act, not offices, or even officers.

The kind of translation into plain English we've been talking about can exert another kind of counterforce, as well. The Official Style, unrelievedly abstract as well as impersonal, echoes the bureaucratic preoccupation with concepts and rules. The Paramedic Method reverses the flow of this current from *concepts* back toward *objects*. It constitutes a ritual reminder to keep our feet on the ground. Dr. Johnson replied to the idealist philosopher's argument that the world exists only in our mind by kicking a stone. The Paramedic Method does much the same kind of thing for us—who's kicking who? The natural gravity of large organizations pulls so strongly toward concepts and abstractions that we need a formulaic counter-ritual. The Paramedic Method provides a start in this direction.

The language of bureaucracy, then, needs a cybernetic circuit to keep its dominant impetus toward impersonality and conceptual generalization in check. It ought to supply negative feedback, not the positive reinforcement provided by The Official Style. Such a counterstatement is not only more attractive and more fun—it's more efficient.

Ego Answers

The "Ego" answers to "Why bother?" come harder than the "Efficiency" arguments because they are so closely invested with questions of morality, sincerity, hypocrisy, and the presentation of self. We might begin to sketch this answer by confronting the temptation head on. Why do all of us moralize so readily about writing style? Writing is usually described in a moral vocabulary—"sincere," "open," "devious," "hypocritical"—but is this vocabulary justified? Why do so many people feel that bad writing threatens the foundations of civilization?

And why, in fact, do we think "bad" the right word to use for it? Why are we seldom content just to call it "inefficient" and let it go at that? Why to "clarity" and "brevity" must we always add a discussion of "sincerity" as well?

Let's start where "sincerity" starts, with the primary ground for morality, the self. We may think of the self as both a dynamic and a static entity. It is static when we think of ourselves as having central, fixed selves independent of our surroundings, an "I" we can remove from society without damage, a central self inside our head. But it becomes dynamic when we think of ourselves as actors playing social roles, a series of roles that vary with the social situations in which we find ourselves. Such a social self amounts to the sum of all the public roles we play. Our complex identity comes from the constant interplay of these two selves. Our final identity is usually a mixed one, few of us being completely the same in all situations or, conversely, social chameleons who change with every context. What allows the self to grow and develop is the free interplay between these two kinds of self, the central self "inside our head" and the social self "out there." If we were completely sincere we would always say exactly what we think—and cause social chaos. If we were always acting an appropriate role, we would be either professional actors or certifiably insane. Reality, for each of us, presents itself as constant oscillation between these two extremes of interior self and social role.

When we say that writing is sincere, we mean that somehow it has managed to express this complex oscillation, this complex self. It has caught the accent of a particular self, a particular mixture of the two selves. Sincerity can't point to any specific verbal configuration, of course, since sincerity varies as widely as people themselves. The sincere writer has not said exactly what she felt in the first words that occur to her. That might produce a revolutionary tirade or "like, you know" conversational babble. Nor has a sincere writer simply borrowed a fixed language, as when a bureaucrat writes in The Official Style. The "sincere" writer has managed to create a style which, like the social self, can become part of society, can work harmoniously in society and, at the same time, like the central self, can represent her unique selfhood. She holds her two selves in balance; this is what "authority" in writing really means.

The act of writing involves for the writer an integration of her self, a deliberate act of balancing its two component parts. It represents an act of socialization, and it is by repeated acts of such socialization that we become sociable beings, that we grow up. Thus the act of writing models the presentation of self in society, constitutes a rehearsal for social reality. It is not simply a question of a preexistent self making its message known to a preexistent society. From the "Ego" point of view, it is not, initially, a question of message at all. Writing is a way to clarify, strengthen, and energize the self, to render individuality rich, full, and social. This does not mean writing that flows, as Terry Southern immortally put it, "right out of the old guts onto the goddamn paper." Just the opposite. Only by taking the position of the reader toward one's own prose, putting a reader's pressure on it, can the self be made to grow. Writing can, through such pressure, enhance and expand the self, allow it to try out new possibilities, tentative selves. We return here to the back pressure revision exerts. It stimulates not only the mind but the whole personality. We are not simply offering an idea but our personality as context for that idea. And just as revision makes our ideas grow and develop, it encourages us to see the different ways we can act in society, the alternative paths to socialize the self.

The moral ingredient in writing, then, works first not on the morality of the message but on the nature of the sender, on the complexity of the self. "Why bother?" To invigorate and enrich your selfhood, to increase, in the most literal sense, your self-consciousness. Writing, properly pursued, does not make you better. It makes you more alive, more coherent, more in control. A mind thinking, not a mind asleep. It aims, that is, not to denature the human relationship that writing sets up, but to enhance and enrich it. It is not trying to squeeze out the expression of personality but to make such expression possible, not trying to obscure all records of a particular occasion and its human relationships but to make them maximally clear. Again, this is why we worry so much about bad writing. It signifies incoherent people, failed social relationships. This worry makes sense only if we feel that writing, ideally, should express human relationships and feelings, not abolish them.

From the "Ego" point of view, then, we revise The Official Style when it fails to socialize the self and hence to enrich it, to discipline the ego to the surrounding egos that give it meaning. This, unhappily, is most of the time. Pure candor can be soundly destructive but so can pure formula, endless cliché. When formula takes over, self and society depart. The joy goes out of the prose. It's no fun to write. And when this happens, you get those social gaffes, those trodden toes, those "failures of communication" that so often interfere with the world's business. The human feeling that has been pushed out the front door sneaks in the back. So when you cease to feel good about what you write, when you cease to add something of yourself to it, watch out!

When we try to put these two answers to "Why bother?" together, we discover a paradoxical convergence. Cases do exist where one answer will do by itself—in the By-Laws case, for example, the "Efficiency" argument really is all we need—but more often than not the two kinds of justification support one another. The "Efficiency" argument, pressed hard enough, comes to overlap the "Ego" argument and vice versa. We may, in this area of overlap, have come across the richness we feel when we use all the customary value-laden terms to describe a piece of prose—"sincere," "honest," "fresh," "straightforward," and so on. We feel that somehow ego and efficiency have come to collaborate in establishing a clarity that makes understanding a pleasure and a shared one.

At this point, the paramedic analogy breaks down. Beyond paramedicine lies medicine; beyond the specific analysis of a specific style—what we have been doing here—lies the study of style in general and its relation to human motive and behavior. Verbal style can no more be fully explained by a set of rules, stylistic or moral, than can any other kind of human behavior. Intuition, trained intuition, figures as strongly in the one as in the other. You must learn how to see.

You'll then be able to answer—situation by situation, one instance at a time, as business decisions are always reached— the fundamental question that this chapter, and this book, can only introduce. How to revise The Official Style is easy, once you know how. As we've seen, anyone can do it. The questions that generate no rules, the questions that try our judgment— and our goodness—are *When?* and *How?* As American business gets bigger and bigger, that is, more hierarchical and bureaucratic, these questions will loom ever larger, and applying the rules will get ever harder. I wish there was an easier answer—a rule for when to apply the rules. But no one has ever found such a touchstone.

When a famous violinist was stopped on the street and asked the way to Carnegie Hall, he replied, "Practice!" Practice is what we have been doing here together in *Revising Business Prose*. And practice shows us the only way from The Official Style to a discourse which does business in a more efficient and humane way.

APPENDIX

TERMS

You can see things you don't know the names for, but in prose style, as in everything else, it is easier to see what you know how to describe. The psychological ease that comes from calling things by their proper names has not often been thought a useful goal by modern pedagogy. As a result, inexperienced writers often find themselves reduced to talking about "smoothness," "flow," and other meaningless generalities when they are confronted by a text. And so here are some basic terms.

PARTS OF SPEECH

In traditional English grammar, there are eight parts of speech: verbs, nouns, pronouns, adjectives, adverbs, prepositions, conjunctions, and interjections. *Grammar*, in its most general sense, refers to all the rules that govern how meaningful statements can be made in any language. *Syntax* refers to sentence structure, to word order. *Diction* means simply word choice. *Usage* means linguistic custom.

Verbs

1. Verbs have two voices, active and passive.
   An *active verb* indicates the subject acting:
   Jack *kicks* Bill.
   A *passive verb* indicates the subject acted upon:
   Bill *is kicked by* Jim.
2. Verbs come in three moods: indicative, subjunctive, and imperative.
   A verb in the *indicative mood* says that something is a fact. If it asks a question, it is a question about a fact:
   Jim kicks Bill. Has Bill kicked Jim yet?
   A verb in the *subjunctive mood* says that something is a wish, hypothetical, or contrary to fact, rather than a fact:
   If Jim *were* clever, he would kick Bill.
   A verb in the *imperative mood* issues a command:
   Jim, *kick* Bill.
3. A verb can be either transitive or intransitive.
   A *transitive verb* takes a direct object:
   Jim *kicks* Bill.
   An *intransitive verb* does not take a direct object. It represents action without a specific goal:
   Lori *runs* every day.
   The verb "to be" ("is," "was," and so on) is often called a *linking verb* because it links subject and predicate without expressing a specific action:
   Elaine *is* a movie mogul.
4. English verbs have six tenses: present, past, present perfect, past perfect, future, and future perfect.
   Present: Jim *kicks* Bill.
   Past: Jim *kicked* Bill.
   Present perfect: Jim *has kicked* Bill.
   Past perfect: Jim *had kicked* Bill.
   Future: Jim *will kick* Bill.
   Future perfect: Jim *will have kicked* Bill.
   The present perfect, past perfect, and future perfect

are called compound tenses. Each tense can have a progressive form (e.g., Present progressive: Jim *is kicking* Bill).

5. Verbs in English have three so-called infinitive forms: *infinitive*, *participle*, and *gerund*. These verb forms often function as adjectives or nouns.

Infinitive:

To assist Elaine isn't easy.

Participles and gerunds have the same form; when the form is used as an adjective, it is called a *participle*, when used as a noun, a *gerund*.

Participles:

Present participle:

Elaine was in an *arguing* mood.

Past participle:

Lori's presentation was very well *argued*.

Gerund:

Arguing with Elaine is no fun.

(When a word separates the "to" in an infinitive from its complementary form, as in "to directly stimulate" instead of "to stimulate," the infinitive is said to be a *split infinitive*. Most people think this separation is something we should avoid if possible.)

Verbs that take "it" or "there" as subjects are said to be in an *impersonal construction*: "It has been decided to fire him" or "There has been a personnel readjustment."

Nouns

A *noun* names something or somebody. A *proper noun* names a particular being or place—Elaine, Pittsburgh.

1. *Number.* The singular number refers to one ("a cat"), plural to more than one ("five cats").
2. *Collective nouns.* Groups may be thought of as a single unit, as in "the army," and thus take a singular verb.

Pronouns

A *pronoun* is a word used instead of a noun. There are different kinds:

1. *Personal pronouns*: I, me, him . . .
2. *Intensive pronouns*: myself, yourself . . .
3. *Relative pronouns*: who, which, that. These must have antecedents, words they refer back to. "Lori has a talent (antecedent) that (relative pronoun) Elaine does not possess."
4. *Indefinite pronouns*: somebody, anybody, anything . . .
5. *Interrogative pronouns*: who?, what?

Adjectives

An *adjective* modifies a noun: "Lori was a *good* hiker."

Adverbs

An *adverb* modifies a verb: "Lori hiked *swiftly* up the trail."

Prepositions

A *preposition* connects a noun or pronoun with a verb, an adjective, or another pronoun: "I ran *into* her arms" or "The girl *with* the blue scarf."

Conjunctions

Conjunctions join sentences or parts of them. There are two kinds, coordinating and subordinating.

1. *Coordinating conjunctions*—and, but, or—connect statements of equal status: "Bill ran *and* Jim fell" or "I got up *but* soon fell down."
2. *Subordinating conjunctions*—that, when, because—con-

nect a main clause with a subordinate one: "I thought *that* they had left."

Interjections

A sudden outcry: "Wow!"

Possessives

Singular: A *worker's* hat. Plural: The *workers'* hats. ("It's," however, equals "it is." **The possessive is "its"—no apostrophe!**)

SENTENCES

Every sentence must have both a subject and verb, stated or implied: "Elaine (subject) directs (verb)."

Three Kinds

1. A *declarative sentence* states a fact: "Elaine directs films."
2. An *interrogative sentence* asks a question: "Does Elaine direct films?"
3. An *exclamatory sentence* registers an exclamation: "Does she ever!"

Three Basic Structures

1. A *simple sentence* makes one self-standing assertion, that is, has one main clause: "Elaine directs films."
2. A *compound sentence* makes two or more self-standing assertions, that is, has two main clauses: "Elaine directs films and Lori is a tax lawyer" or "Jim kicks Bill and Bill feels it and Bill kicks Jim back."
3. A *complex sentence* makes one self-standing assertion and one or more dependent assertions in the form of

subordinate clauses dependent on the main clause: "Elaine, who has just finished directing *Jim Kicks Bill*, must now consult Lori about her tax problems before she can start blocking out *Being Kicked: The Sequel*."

In *compound sentences*, the clauses are connected by *coordinating conjunctions*; in *complex sentences*, by *subordinating conjunctions*.

Restrictive and Nonrestrictive Relative Clauses

A *restrictive clause* modifies directly, and so restricts the meaning of the antecedent it refers back to: "This is the tire *that blew out on the freeway*." One specific tire is referred to. In such clauses the relative clause is not set off by a comma.

A *nonrestrictive clause*, though still a dependent clause, does not directly modify its antecedent and is set off by commas. "These tires, *which are quite expensive*, never blow out on the freeway."

Appositives

An *appositive* is an amplifying word or phrase placed next to the term it refers to and set off by commas: "Henry VIII, *a glutton for punishment*, rode out hunting even when sick and in pain."

BASIC SENTENCE PATTERNS

What words do you use to describe the basic syntactic patterns in a sentence? In addition to the basic types, declarative, interrogative, and exclamatory, and the basic forms of simple, compound, and complex, other terms sometimes come in handy.

Parataxis and Hypotaxis

Parataxis: Phrases or clauses arranged independently, in a coordinate construction, and often without connectives (e.g., "I came, I saw, I conquered").

Hypotaxis: Phrases or clauses arranged in a dependent subordinate relationship (e.g., "I came, and after I came and looked around a bit, I decided, well, why not, and so conquered").

The adjectival forms are *paratactic* and *hypotactic* (e.g., "Hemingway favors a paratactic syntax while Faulkner prefers a hypotactic one").

Asyndeton and Polysyndeton

Asyndeton: Connectives are omitted between words, phrases, or clauses (e.g., "I've been stressed, distressed, beat down, beat up, held down, held up, conditioned, reconditioned").

Polysyndeton: Connectives are always supplied between words and phrases, or clauses, as when Milton talks about Satan pursuing his way, "And swims, or sinks, or wades, or creeps, or flies."

The adjectives are *asyndetic* and *polysyndetic*.

Periodic Sentence

A *periodic sentence* is a long sentence with a number of elements, usually balanced or antithetical, standing in a clear syntactical relationship to each other. Usually it suspends the conclusion of the sense until the end of the sentence, and so is sometimes said to use a *suspended syntax*. A perfect example is the passage from Lord Brougham's defense of Queen Caroline quoted in Chapter 3 of this book's companion volume, *Revising Prose*. A periodic sentence shows us a pattern of thought that has been fully worked out, whose power relationships of subordination have been carefully determined, and whose timing has been climactically ordered. In a periodic sentence, the mind has finished working on the thought, left it fully formed.

There is no equally satisfactory antithetical term for the opposite kind of sentence, a sentence whose elements are loosely related to one another, follow in no particularly antithetical climactic order, and do not suspend its grammatical completion until the close. Such a style is often called a *running style* or a *loose style*, but the terms remain pretty vague. The loose style, we can say, often reflects a mind *in the process of thinking* rather than, as in the periodic sentence, having already completely ordered its thinking. A sentence so loose as to verge on incoherence, grammatical or syntactical, is often called a *run-on sentence.*

Isocolon

The Greek word *isocolon* means, literally, syntactic units of equal length, and it is used in English to describe the repetition of phrases of equal length and corresponding structure. Preachers, for example, often depend on isocolon to build up a rhythmic pattern or develop a series of contrasting ideas. Falstaff parodies this habit in Shakespeare's *1 Henry IV*: "Well, God give *thee the spirit of persuasion* and *him the ears of profiting,* that *what thou speakest may move* and *what he hears may be believed,* that *the true prince* may, for recreation sake, prove *a false thief.*" And later in the play, "Harry, now I do *not* speak to thee *in drink but in tears, not in pleasure but in passion, not in words only, but in woes also.*"

Chiasmus

Chiasmus is the basic pattern of antithetical inversion, the AB:BA pattern. President John Kennedy used it in his inaugural address:

A	**B**
Ask not *what your country*	*can do for you*, but
B	**A**
what you can do	*for your country.*

Anaphora

When you begin a series of phrases, clauses, or sentences with the same word or phrase, you are using *anaphora*. So Shakespeare's Henry V to some henchpersons who have betrayed him:

> Show men dutiful?
> *Why, so didst thou.* Seem they grave and learned?
> *Why, so didst thou.* Come they of noble family?
> *Why, so didst thou.* Seem they religious?
> *Why, so didst thou.*
>
> (*Henry V*, II, ii)

Tautology

Repetition of the same idea in different words. In many ways, The Official Style is founded on this pattern. Here's a neat example from Shakespeare:

> *Lepidus.* What manner o'thing is your crocodile?
> *Antony.* It is shap'd, sir, like itself, and it is as broad as it has breadth. It is just so high as it is, and moves with its own organs. It lives by that which nourisheth it, and the elements once out of it, it transmigrates.
> *Lepidus.* What colour is it of?
> *Antony.* Of its own colour too.
> *Lepidus.* 'Tis a strange serpent.
> *Antony.* 'Tis so. And the tears of it are wet.
>
> (*Antony and Cleopatra*, II, vii)

NOUN STYLE AND VERB STYLE

Every sentence must have a noun and a verb, but one can be emphasized, sometimes almost to the exclusion of the other. The Official Style—strings of prepositional phrases + "is"—

exemplifies a noun style *par excellence*. Here are three examples, the first of a noun style, the second of a verb style, and the third of a balanced noun-verb mixture.

Noun Style

There is in turn a two-fold structure of this "binding-in." In the first place, by virtue of internalization of the standard, conformity with it tends to be of personal, expressive and/or instrumental significance to ego. In the second place, the structuring of the reactions of alter to ego's action as sanctions is a function of his conformity with the standard. Therefore conformity as a direct mode of the fulfillment of his own need-dispositions tends to coincide with the conformity as a condition of eliciting the favorable and avoiding the unfavorable reactions of others.

(Talcott Parsons, *The Social System* [Glencoe, Ill.: Free Press, 1951], p. 38.)

Verb Style

Patrols, sweeps, missions, search and destroy. It continued every day as if part of sunlight itself. I went to the colonel's briefings every day. He explained how effectively we were keeping the enemy off balance, not allowing them to move in, set up mortar sites, and gather for attack. He didn't seem to hate them. They were to him like pests or insects that had to be kept away. It seemed that one important purpose of patrols was just for them to take place, to happen, to exist; there had to be patrols. It gave the men something to do. Find the enemy, make contact, kill, be killed, and return. Trap, block, hold. In the first five days, I lost six corpsmen—two killed, four wounded.

(John A. Parrish, *12, 20 & 5: A Doctor's Year in Vietnam* [Baltimore: Penguin Books, 1973], p. 235.)

Mixed Noun-Verb Style

We know both too much and too little about Louis XIV ever to succeed in capturing the whole man. In externals, in the mere business of eating, drinking, and dressing, in the outward routine of what he loved to call the *métier du roi*, no historical character, not even Johnson or Pepys, is better known to us; we can even, with the aid of his own writings, penetrate a little of the majestic facade which is Le Grand Roi. But when we have done so, we see as in a glass darkly. Hence the extraordinary number and variety of judgments which have been passed upon him; to one school, he is incomparably the ablest ruler in modern European history; to another, a mediocre blunderer, pompous, led by the nose by a succession of generals and civil servants; whilst to a third, he is no great king, but still the finest actor of royalty the world has ever seen.

(W. H. Lewis, *The Splendid Century: Life in the France of Louis XIV* [New York: Anchor Books, 1953], p. 1.)

PATTERNS OF RHYTHM AND SOUND

Meter

The terms used for scanning (marking the meter of) poetry sometimes prove useful for prose as well.

> *iamb*: unstressed syllable followed by a stressed one (e.g., in vólve).
> *trochee*: opposite of iamb (e.g., ám ber).
> *anapest*: two unstressed syllables and one stressed syllable (e.g., there he góes).
> *dactyl*: opposite of anapest, one stressed syllable followed by two unstressed ones (e.g., óp er ate).

These patterns form *feet*. If a line contains two, it is a *dimeter*; three, a *trimeter*; four, a *tetrameter*; five, a *pentameter*; six, a *hexameter*. The adjectival forms are *iambic*, *trochaic*, *anapestic*, and *dactylic*.

Sound Resemblances

Alliteration: This originally meant the repetition of initial consonant sounds but came to mean repetition of consonant sounds wherever they occurred, and now is often used to indicate vowel-sound repetition (also called assonance) as well. You can use it as a general term for this kind of sound play: "Peter Piper picked a peck of pickled peppers"; "Bill will always swill his fill."

Homoioteleuton: This jawbreaker refers, in Latin, to words with similar endings, usually case endings. An English analogy would be "looked" and "booked." You can use it for cases like this, to describe, for example, the "shun" words—"function," "organization," "facilitation"—and the sound clashes they cause.

For further explanation of the basic terms of grammar, see George O. Curme's *English Grammar* in the Barnes & Noble College Outline Series. For a fuller discussion of rhetorical terms like *chiasmus* and *asyndeton*, see Richard A. Lanham's *A Handlist of Rhetorical Terms*, 2nd ed., University of California Press, 1991. For a fuller discussion of prose style, see Richard A. Lanham's *Analyzing Prose*, Macmillan/Scribner's, 1983.

INDEX